Praise for **The Financially Savvy Entrepreneur**:

"I can't believe there is an actual book about money that I can relate to *and* that makes me chuckle. Emily's book is actually easy for a money-avoider like me to understand, and I love her personality. She is relatable, the information is easy to absorb, and as far as helpful... let's just say I finally understand how I can take care of my business like a true CEO. Every entrepreneur needs to read this book, and as soon as humanly possible."

—Jessica Kupferman, digital business and branding strategist and host of Lady Business Radio

"Interviewing over 500 of the world's most successful and inspiring entrepreneurs has taught me many things. One theme that continues to arise during our "failure" segment is how so many entrepreneurs fail to control their money *while* focusing on running a business. Emily's book needs to become the bible for entrepreneurs who know they will face this challenge, and I could not shower more glowing praise on how many "failures" will be avoided by applying the principles **The Financially Savvy Entrepreneur** champions."

—John Lee Dumas, host of Entrepreneur on Fire

"Emily Chase Smith's **The Financially Savvy Entrepreneur** should be required reading for anyone starting a small business. Chase Smith's years of helping entrepreneurs in financial hot water have given her excellent insight into how those of us building our businesses on the fly can avoid being a poster child for the consequences of financial ignorance. Until I read this book, I had no idea we were making such potentially dangerous mistakes, much less how to solve them. With kindness, calm, and good humor, Chase Smith offers a set of very practical tools and common-sense solutions that offer a clear, direct path out of the wilderness of small business finance."

—Yolanda O'Bannon, co-owner, YoWangdu Tibetan Culture

"I find it a little scary (okay, more than a little) that many entrepreneurs focus on the wrong things...from 495,881-page business plans to the flashiest Websites in the universe, when at the end of the day, a successful entrepreneur is a profitable one. Emily will get you on the path to profitability (*without* being bored) in **The Financially Savvy Entrepreneur**. Not only is it a must-read, it's also a must-remember and a must-follow."

—David Siteman Garland, creator of The Rise to the Top

THE
FINANCIALLY
SAVVY
ENTREPRENEUR

THE
FINANCIALLY
SAVVY
ENTREPRENEUR

Navigate the Money Maze
of Running a Business

Emily Chase Smith, Esq.

CAREER
PRESS
Pompton Plains, N.J.

THE FINANCIALLY SAVVY ENTREPRENEUR
EDITED AND TYPESET BY KARA KUMPEL
Cover design by Rob Johnson
Printed in the U.S.A.

To order this title, please call toll-free 1-800-CAREER-1 (NJ and Canada: 201-848-0310) to order using VISA or MasterCard, or for further information on books from Career Press.

The Career Press, Inc.
220 West Parkway, Unit 12
Pompton Plains, NJ 07444
www.careerpress.com

Library of Congress Cataloging-in-Publication Data
Smith, Emily Chase.
  The financially savvy entrepreneur : navigate the money maze of running a business / by Emily Chase Smith, Esq.
    pages cm
  Includes index.
  ISBN 978-1-60163-317-0 -- ISBN 978-1-60163-469-6 (ebook) 1.
New business enterprises--Finance. 2. Small business--Finance. 3. Entrepreneurship. I. Title.

  HG4027.6.S644 2014
  658.15--dc23

                    2014000409

All books start as dreams, even non-fiction financial ones, and belief is the nourishment the dream needs to become reality. Thank you to my family, Chandler, Genevieve, Constance, and Ambrose, and BFF Kristie for nourishing this dream. I love you all.

Contents

Preface:

Entrepreneurs Are a Different Animal

Are You Susan?

Susan had been in business two years. It had been a wild ride, but she had put in the hours of toil and was well on her way to the big prize. She had designed, focused, and then refined her product, her marketing, her social media, and her staffing, again and again. This wasn't her first rodeo. As a serial entrepreneur, she was driven and wise. She had rising sales and a strong team. So why was Susan sitting in my office holding a Summons and Complaint, looking like her dog just died?

Susan's not a real person; she's many real people. She's a composite of entrepreneur client after entrepreneur client I've had in my law practice, looking for help, wondering if it's all over just when it finally looks like it's begun. These entrepreneurs need my help when, just as the product, systems, and people are in place, the hammer drops, and no amount of retooling or drive is going to pull their plane out of its tailspin.

Who We Are as Entrepreneurs

We entrepreneurs—and I do count myself among them—are optimists by nature. We have a solid-to-the-core belief that we can create something out of nothing. We've decided to exit the mainstream, eschewing "secure" jobs, steady work hours, and the golden pocket watch of retirement to live lives that swing between the pits of despair and the heights of elation. We have a "type" and a set of characteristics as unifying as any in the wild kingdom. Either we are suffering from collective delusion or we are truly the visionaries we consider ourselves to be.

Whatever the mind can conceive and
believe, the mind can achieve.

—Dr. Napoleon Hill

We entrepreneurs ignore conventional wisdom on every front. We're visionaries following the road less traveled. We've concluded the mainstream world has little to offer us, and we gravitate toward others who believe the same. We have trouble holding conversations with the traditionally employed at polite dinner parties because we feel that work is something to be enjoyed, explored, and expanded, not something to be complained about. If, at that same dinner party, we're introduced to a fellow entrepreneur, the night passes in a blink. Despite differences in gender, age, or industry, our entrepreneurial souls connect and there is no shortage of topics to survey.

If you and I found ourselves sitting near each other enjoying a hearty bowl of soup as a first course, I know we'd get along smashingly. I don't know you, but I know you—if you know what I mean. We're simpatico even though I'm a 43-year-old mother of three who loves to surf and travel and couldn't tell you who played in the last Super Bowl.

Not long ago at a Las Vegas convention for bloggers and podcasters known as New Media Expo, I had a rousing round-table discussion with a group of young, single, twenty-something "boys." We should have had nothing in common (see my aforementioned demographics), and yet we did. The conversation ended because, this being Vegas, they were off to party, and there our differences became apparent: I'm a teetotaler who was ready to turn in for the night. But right up to that point, we were totally in sync. They are entrepreneurs, and so am I. In contrast, when I sit chatting with a group of 40-ish mothers in my neighborhood schoolyard, my eyes glaze over. We have nothing in common, even though, on paper, it looks as if we should. Really, if I have to hear about potty training one more time, I'm going to stick a fork in my eye. I think what makes us entrepreneurs fast friends is that we face the same struggles and experience the same successes. We are the same animal, on the same savannah, trying to take down the same zebra.

At the aforementioned New Media Expo, I attended a keynote speech given by Dana White of UFC fame. In truth, I didn't want to be there, but I had gone along for the ride before finding out who the speaker was. As Dana White was introduced, I had to look up what "UFC" was on my iPhone—I really had no idea. When I read the first sentence of the Wikipedia entry, if I hadn't been pretty much front and center in the audience, I would have snuck out and engaged in some non-alcoholic libations. Wikipedia says Dana White is: "...an American businessman, entrepreneur, and the President of mixed martial arts organization the Ultimate Fighting Championship (UFC), based in the U.S." I'm glad I couldn't sneak out, because Dana White proceeded to give the most fascinating keynote I've ever heard (and I'm no keynote slacker). He's a businessman and entrepreneur first. He's also a former boxer and someone you most definitely don't want to mess with. How can you not respect someone with the vision to make something out of nothing? And when he verbally smacked down some audience commentators it only added to his appeal.

Despite what a demographic profile might claim, I have much more in common with Dana White and the twenty-something single boys than do I with my local neighborhood mothers. As a result, in finances, along with many other subjects, advice and direction that's designed for my neighbors holds little to no help for me. My neighbors don't live on a savannah; they live in a forest. They don't chase down gazelle; they graze on berries. Instruction on how to best climb a redwood helps me not at all.

Why This Book?

Members of the entrepreneur species share common financial challenges, and there is little in the bookstore to help guide our financial journey that reflects the financial realities of our lives. Whereas enough has been written on the subject of budgets, saving, debt, retirement, and so on to fell a large forest, it does not address the unique situation of entrepreneurs. Entrepreneurs are generally relegated to a footnote that sounds something like, "If you have irregular income, plan for fluctuations." It's like telling that lion on the savannah to plan for irregular zebra. Gee, thanks for the tip. I'll get right on that.

There are fundamental differences between an entrepreneur and an employed person that go far past a fluctuating income:

- An employed person isn't responsible for anyone outside his immediate family. An entrepreneur often supports many people and their extended families.

- An employed person isn't responsible for supplying the tools necessary for work like office space, computers, tech support, supplies, and phone service. An entrepreneur is.

- An employed person is paid first. An entrepreneur is paid last, if at all.

- An employed person is paid whether or not the business is successful, and oftentimes despite poor performance. An entrepreneur is paid only when the business makes money consistently and when she is performing at the highest levels.

- An employed person doesn't make payments on money borrowed to support his employment. An entrepreneur often makes personal payments on money borrowed to begin or continue the business.

⅄ An employed person can quit a job anytime and move on. An entrepreneur can't. The business and personal finances of an entrepreneur are often so intertwined that the entrepreneur must soldier on, even after the thrill is gone.

The differences are so significant that a book written to a 9-to-5-er can't even begin to address the reality of an entrepreneur.

Who Am I?

Why should you listen to me? What makes me the Entrepreneur's Money Expert (besides the fact that I can consistently spell *entrepreneur* correctly)? You might be surprised to know that I do not hail from the land of accounting. I'm not a CPA and I don't have an MBA with a concentration in finance. In fact, I'm from a field I've been told is much more akin to root canal work or getting a mammogram—bankruptcy law.

After my requisite years practicing "food law"—in other words, whatever would put food on the table—I chose to focus on bankruptcy because it's an area of the law where you can find someone in a tough place and put him in a better one. Along the way I attracted a lot of entrepreneurs and small business owners in financial trouble, and in fact they were my favorite clientele. After years of helping entrepreneurs off the financial rocks, I found myself something of a zealot. No longer was I happy to help improve the life of one person at a time; I wanted to prevent all entrepreneurs from hitting the rocks in the first place. I wanted to be a lighthouse, not the Coast Guard.

This book, along with my podcast and blog, is what I want to tell you from my vantage point at the top of the lighthouse while you navigate the rocky coastline of business. The knowledge sweet spot we're hitting here is akin to brushing your teeth: you need to get the job done, but it shouldn't take up too much of your time or be too complicated. You need a system you can employ on a daily basis to move you from being scared and making crap up as you go to being confident and financially savvy.

What You'll Find Here

In the pages of this book, you'll find both preventive medicine and cures. This book will advise you on how to avoid the pitfalls and survive the dips. We'll start with looking at where you are now in your financial journey. Then I'll discuss important pivots to make and check-and-balance systems to put in place. Then I'll teach you how to get out of a tight jam. The goal is to make your current business as successful as possible and to make you a financially savvy entrepreneur who will bring that savvy to every business you touch.

The good news is that you're here. So settle in, learn, plan, and execute. Bring your business brain and entrepreneur's heart, and together we'll make sure your business and personal finances thrive.

Introduction:
When the Sheriff Comes a-Knockin'

In the Preface you met Susan, an amalgamation of my bankruptcy clients. You may or may not relate to Susan, sitting in my office holding a Summons and Complaint. You may have asked, *How was she sued if she has a successful business? Further, even if she was sued, why is that the end of the world? How could this ever happen to me?*

Let me flesh out Susan's all-too-common scenario. As I mentioned, Susan's an experienced entrepreneur who's been in business two years with rising sales and strong staff. Susan started her retail brick-and-mortar business with one location. That location did well, so, on the strength of her business model, she scouted and opened two additional locations using the same strategy. Dreams of franchising dancing in her head, she signed three-year leases on each of the new locations, did tenant improvements, and ran.

As the months went on, Susan noticed that although her original location and the second location were doing well, her third store wasn't flying. Never one to give up, Susan threw the full weight of her creativity and money into advertising and promotions, but alas, location #3 never lived up to expectations. Susan knew it was bad, but wasn't quite sure how bad. She wasn't a "financial person," she was a creative. After a painful year and a half of hustling and spending, Susan conceded location #3 was never going to be the success that its big brothers were. With a heavy heart Susan decided it was time to stop the bloodletting and close location #3.

Susan's landlord didn't have quite the same perspective. Bloodletting or not, the landlord had in his hand a signed lease with a personal guarantee for three years at $4,000 a month. When Susan closed the store and stopped paying the rent, the landlord sued both the business and Susan personally for the entire amount due under the lease: two years and six months at $4,000 a month, adding up to $120,000, plus costs, attorney fees, and interest. The landlord also demanded that the building be returned to its original configuration before the tenant improvements, per the requirements of the lease. A uniformed sheriff served the lawsuit papers to Susan at home, in full view of her husband and kids. Susan is successful with her other two locations, but not successful enough to write a six-figure check.

The papers served to Susan decreed that the lawsuit must be answered in 30 days. In other words, within 30 days Susan needed to find and hire an attorney to defend her against a lawsuit for which there is really no defense—after all, she did sign the lease, and now she's not paying it. They further stated that if Susan fails to respond, the landlord gets a judgment for the entire amount, which will be good for 10 years and renewable for 10-year terms.

Then, Susan got another kick in the teeth. She had used her personal savings and all of her retirement to fund the business. She had also used business credit cards to finance the tenant improvements on the second and third locations. Now she can't make the payments on the credit cards. Susan thought the credit cards were business cards, because they had the business name on them, but they were also personally guaranteed by Susan (as almost all business credit cards are). She now has to deal with a second lawsuit, from the creditors, and this one is also against the business and her personally.

As Susan sits in my office and lays out the situation, she's struck by the enormity. She's out of money
and out of credit. She has no income source. Susan
wonders how she's going to make her house payment
or even buy food at the grocery store.

Stop Singing Sad Songs

I hate to start out this book with such a downer
story. I would prefer to play happy music, but Susan
represents an all-too-common plight of entrepreneurs.
When we focus on the marketing, the product, and the
locations, but not on the financial structure and financial health of the business, we can kill an otherwise
strong business. We can have a successful business
concept and end up right where Susan is, wondering
what to tell the people who rely on us.

Let's sing a happier tune. Let's take Susan's tale
from a sad country song to bubblegum pop. Let's back-
track and bestow upon Susan some financial savvy. In
this version of events, before expanding into new locations Susan has first created an exit plan (Chapter
5) that guides her in deciding how far she's willing
to ride the train. It marks her exit from the business
and makes sure to leave her and her family something
to live on and a platform from which to start her next
venture. With this exit strategy she will never get to
the point at which she's completely out of money. With
this financial savvy, Susan has been careful to keep

her business and personal financial life completely and legally separate. In fact, she's gone back and unwound some interlocking pieces left over from her start-up days by negotiating with her landlords to remove her as a personal guarantor of the leases (Chapter 10). She has converted credit card debt to a business line of credit tied only to the business (Chapter 11), and paid off much of it.

Susan has a system for generating financial statements and reviewing those statements with regular brainstorming sessions (Chapter 3)—no more desk and floor covered with floating paper. She knows when it's wise to launch additional locations and how to launch them so that one location doesn't jeopardize the rest. She makes wise tenant-improvement decisions based on what the business can support (Chapter 4). Susan knows when to pivot or make changes because she has her finger on the financial pulse of the business (Chapter 3). She is clear on the risk of each decision and makes the decision with eyes wide open. She knows how to direct her cash flow when times are tight to bridge a gap (Chapter 7). She doesn't reach the point of debt negotiation (Chapter 10) or bankruptcy (Chapter 11) because Susan is a rock star—a financially savvy rock star.

This is a much happier story. Let's make this one yours.

Your Story

Where do you fit in the entrepreneurial spectrum? Are you a young whippersnapper with a big idea and even bigger cajones? Are you a mother with children, making it happen during school hours, at the McDonald's play yard, and when the babysitter's there? Are you an encore entrepreneur, with one successful career in the can and a lifetime's worth of ideas ready to launch? Are you coming home, stripping off the suit, and working your side hustle into fulltime cash?

No matter where you are on your journey, you need financial savvy. It can be disastrous not to have it—and the next best thing to heaven when you get it right. Financial savvy will take your million-dollar idea and actually put a million dollars in your pocket. It will make all your hard work worthwhile.

You will find your financial groove within these pages. Your investment in your education and entrepreneurial chops here will serve you long after your current entrepreneurial venture goes down in the record books. Your entrepreneurial savvy will set you up for success time and time again.

Eighty percent of business start-ups are self-funded or bootstrapped. Businesses are started with a dream and a scheme to solve a problem, create a new product or service, or fill a hole in the marketplace. Think back to your start-up days (or think about right now if that's where you are). Ideas danced in your head at all hours, glorious, energy-fueled and terror striking all at the same time. You and your vision were going to change the world. Statues would be erected, sonnets written, magazine covers graced. With a vision that big, a gift the world was waiting for, any measures necessary must be taken.

To push that dream into reality, you needed cash. Maybe not a lot, but some. You were like a Jr. High girl that just has to have that dress for the dance. You'd do anything to get what you want, but, to your chagrin, you found that venture capitalists and angel investors are not as common as *Entrepreneur Magazine* makes it seem. Almost never is there a smiling venture capitalist with a blank check at your door. But we are entrepreneurs, we are savannah lions. We will have our zebras. In your hunt, did you:

- ⅄ Use savings
- ⅄ Sell stuff
- ⅄ Use retirement funds
- ⅄ Borrow from friends
- ⅄ Borrow from family
- ⅄ Have family borrow from their retirement or home equity
- ⅄ Use credit cards
- ⅄ Apply for new credit cards to use
- ⅄ Use other people's credit cards
- ⅄ Make nice with the local loan shark

Most of us draw the line at clearly unlawful activity, but, like an addict, we entrepreneurs will pull out all the stops to make the dream a reality. This is the anatomy of a start-up. Financially, as entrepreneurs, many of us never move past the start-up mentality of taking what we have, which is never quite enough, and making it work. From the beginning and through the lean times, we get creative, financially and otherwise. This is our baby and it cannot fail. *We* cannot fail. We will make it work. And we do. Out of nothing, we create a living, breathing business that provides value to the world and provides us with an income and freedom. But start-up mentality only gets us so far. Continuing to think like a Jr. High girl going to a dance becomes less attractive once you're out of Jr. High. It's like a decades-long cheeseburger-and-fries habit: You can get away with it while you're young, but as you approach 40, something's got to change.

Let's draw a parallel from our cheeseburger-and-fries to a healthy, mature, vegetable-fueled business. That business stands on its own. It knows its numbers. It makes wise, reasoned decisions. It doesn't shoot from the hip. Can that be done if you're using the anything-goes method I just described? Surely not. Until your business is weaned from cheeseburgers to Brussels sprouts, it's not a viable, healthy business: it's a financial mess waiting to rear its ugly head, and when it does that cholesterol will kill your business, your personal finances, and anything else in its path.

Business Beyond Start-Up: A Story of Moving from Cheeseburgers to Brussels Sprouts

Let's meet David (name and details changed to protect client confidentiality). When I met him, it was a hat-in-hands moment. He came in clutching the dreaded credit-card Summons and Complaint, served, as always, at home in full view of the wife and kids. Like so many entrepreneurs (but not you, dear reader, very soon), the sins of David's start-up days haunted him. Let's look at his business before he earned his savvy.

David serviced the medical profession. He had a small office, two full-time staff members, and his wife did the books. His income from the business and from what he paid his wife supported his family.

Lawsuits don't happen in a vacuum. There was a reason David was on the receiving end of one. As I discussed with David, to address only the lawsuit and not the underlying issues wouldn't be doing him any favors. Sure, we could settle the lawsuit, but that wouldn't take care of the structural issues that brought him to my door in the first place. To address those, I needed to know (and David needed to recognize):

- What other potential monsters could David expect to see in the near future?
- How entangled were David's business and personal finances?

⅄ Did David have a good handle on his business metrics?

⅄ How was David making business decisions, from the hip or using a system?

⅄ Could we get David on a long-term sustainable path allowing him to win in both his business and personal life?

When we began to unpack David's situation, the first thing we found is that he could not answer some pretty basic financial questions about his business, like gross income, net income, monthly payroll commitment, and debt load. David's answers came with caveats such as, "I think," "There is that one loan...," "I'm not sure," and "Let me get back to you on that." David clearly did not have his finger on the pulse of his business.

Interestingly, like most entrepreneurs I consult with, David could answer questions about the products and services he provided in great detail, providing a long discourse about why they were more effective, more environmentally friendly, and longer lasting than his competitors'. He had statistics at the ready and could field any question with aplomb. However, as soon as the conversation steered to anything financial, he was at a loss.

I discovered that David relied on his wife, his in-house bookkeeper, to "do the books." David's wife is a very nice lady, but she had no financial background.

(Her educational background and her professional expertise were in the area of family counseling.) She now saw clients part-time, raised the kids, and did David's books on the side.

David had an LLC in place and had complied with all the formalities, and relied heavily on his CPA for financial advice, but only as it pertained to tax savings. He and his CPA met only a few times a year and only to figure out how to maximize his tax savings. If David was dealing with a financial issue that went beyond tax consequences, he handled it himself—or didn't handle it. David carried a large Accounts Receivable, and he did some of his work on "spec," and would get paid, or not, depending on factors completely outside his control.

As we unpacked David's scenario, it became abundantly clear that the lawsuit was a symptom of a much larger problem. Although David had a great product and good business systems, if he continued neglecting the financial side of the business he would be a successful failure. His financial laissez faire attitude would not carry him into the next phase of a successful business.

Although it may appear otherwise, all businesses are run by people. As David and I talked, some other contributing factors became apparent: He had an advanced degree and graduated at the top of his class. He was an academic rock star. On top of his book smarts, he had designed and launched a product that was very much in demand in his region. As the business grew, the demands of his family life grew right alongside it. The stunning house, dialed cars, private school, and swanky vacations required a sizeable income to support.

David may be in the medical business, but I wrote the prescription. Here's what we did to turn up David's financial savvy.

⅄ **Step 1:** We released David's wife from her accountancy duties, giving her the flexibility she needed to focus on her therapy clients and family. In her place David hired an off-site bookkeeper who charged a very reasonable $30 per hour. It was more than David was paying his wife, but the bookkeeper had extensive knowledge and experience and did the job in half the time—really, half!

⅄ **Step 2:** Using reports his bookkeeper generated, David spent an hour each week looking at the financial markers in his business. He specifically looked at where his income originated and how he spent it. As a result of that weekly hour, David made some significant changes in the way he ran his business. He dialed way back on the "spec" work. It was scary to let go of potential clients and their income, but after reviewing the reports carefully, he realized that he was so infrequently compensated for that time, it was wiser to give it up and focus on more valuable clients. David used the time he was no longer working on "spec" clients to network and market the business. It wasn't long before those efforts paid off and David saw that, too, in his profit and loss (P&L). After the first few months, David had a set direction. He reduced his quality time with the P&L to once a month, but he often found himself reviewing it at other times when he had a business decision to make.

David kept his current CPA, but realized the limitations of the advice he would receive there. He was more realistic about what to expect from the CPA and knew that he, David, was the real financial driver of the business— that's not something you can outsource, even to a professional.

⋏ **Step 3:** Because we knew his business and personal finances hadn't transcended the start-up phase, we looked at every outstanding liability and commitment of the business. What we found surprised David, but not me. David and his business were one. As one went, so would the other. We embarked on a course to separate the two. When the lease on David's office came up for renewal, he negotiated the next term with the business as the only signatory to the lease. David opened up a line of credit at the local bank and shifted the debt on the business to the new line of credit. That took some time because he carried heavy personal and business debt, but as he was intimately familiar with his P&L he was able to make the business more profitable. With the extra income, he first paid off the debts for which he had personal liability. In a few years David and his business were separate and he was free to build wealth independent of the business.

⋏ **Step 4:** This step was tough because it involved a hard look at David's personal finances. The decisions he made here would involve his whole family—a family which, by now, was accustomed to a certain standard of living. David was carrying more than a million dollars in debt on his personal residence. The income required to service this was staggering. Paying the million-dollar mortgage was only the start. Of course the house is in an area with high property taxes and homeowner's association fees. Gardeners and cleaners are common, and one can hardly park a 10-year-old Honda in the driveway. David had about $13 to $14,000 a month tied up in paying for the family's house alone.

It took some time, but David and his family were able to make some lifestyle changes that (although painful at the time) they now say were pivotal to their happiness as a family.

They moved to a smaller house (a decisive change that took courage) and traded down their cars. The kids stayed in private school because that was important to them as a family, but they dialed down some of their lifestyle choices.

As I see time and time again, David's entrepreneurial juices really started flowing once he was released from that large nut he needed to bring home each month. He was able to keep more money in the business and develop some new lines of business that moved him in an even more profitable direction. Interestingly, they never moved back to the ritzy neighborhood.

➤ **Step 5:** The lawsuit was the pain point David presented, but in the end it was anticlimactic. I knew the creditor was (understandably) not eager to litigate, and David certainly didn't want to either. We settled the lawsuit within a few weeks, and David didn't even have to answer it.

I tell you David's story because no matter where you sit as you read this book, both literally and figuratively, you need to see the goal line. The road can be long. Note that we didn't solve all David's problems in the span of a 30-minute sitcom episode. David put in the work, he changed the way he looked at his business, he made the tough decisions, and he and his family made sacrifices. I can convey to you that David regrets none of it. In fact, he views the lawsuit that started the ball rolling as a gift to him. It was the gift of motivation, resulting in changes to his business that led directly to dramatic improvement in his feelings of satisfaction about his personal and family life. It was a game changer.

In the many years I've dealt with the inner workings of entrepreneurs' finances, I've seen the recovery of many businesses similar to Susan's and David's. The Susans and Davids have told me things they've told no one else. There have been tears. It's been tough, but with it has come the opportunity to move past the sins of our start-up past and on to success.

Wherever you are in your evolution as an entrepreneur, there are choices to be made that will have a direct impact on your future. You can continue to ride the train you're on. You can do the same thing you've always done. You can continue to focus all your energy on the nuts and bolts of your business and ignore the underlying financial realities. *Or*, you can learn to be a financially savvy entrepreneur who does as David did: learn what you need to know, make the tough decisions, and execute to create a strong financial base from which to grow your business as big and tall and wide as you can dream.

Put another way, we can live as sad David, happy David, or clueless David. Notice you're still David in all the scenarios. David still has the same business, he's just thinking about it differently, and that mindset changes the way he operates. He moves from sad David to happy David with just a few pivots, and those pivots change his whole game forever and ever. Sad David is in my office with a Summons and Complaint. Happy David is financially savvy, and as a result is on a beach drinking fruity drinks. This book is the road map. The road map is mine, but the choice is yours.

Chapter 1:
The Runway Equation

The Runway, and Its Friendly Companion, Baselining

The constant concern of entrepreneurs is that we'll run out of money before we can make our business idea a reality. We face this at the beginning of a business venture and several times throughout its life as we jump from tree to tree in the quest for the top. This is what keeps us up at night. Money worries sap our creativity and dampen our drive.

And it's not only the money to run the business we need to worry about; it's also money to run our lives while we build the business. As we saw in the Introduction, we are not 9-to-5-ers who receive a paycheck from the top floor. We eat what we kill, and we need to kill enough to feed ourselves, our families, and our business. That's a lot of zebra.

The concept of the runway is something I first discovered on The Lifestyle Business Podcast, from lifestyle entrepreneurs and those who write about lifestyle design. It provides a great framework for the idea of how long you can continue down a path before running out of time or money. It's modeled on the idea of the amount of runway an airplane needs in order to take off: With enough runway a plane can get into the air. Without enough, you have a tragic situation.

The idea of the runway is best understood in the context of the lifestyle entrepreneur's reality: that of a twenty-something straight out of college, with big dreams. So picture yourself at the beginning of your working life, with all your entrepreneurial zest, but none of your hard-learned lessons. Now take away all ties to the physical world except for the love of your family. Now you have no encumbrances, but you also don't have the resources you may have come to rely upon—no savings, no 401k, no home equity. As you fashion your life from scratch, what would you do to launch your big dream? Eating ramen noodles, the staple of college students the world round, comes immediately to mind. As a free bird you might rent a small apartment in a less-than-desirable area of town. If you were really hardcore you might couch-surf your way to nearly zero overhead. Your car would be sold or downgraded to the bare minimum. Meat might not grace your plate for weeks. This type of lifestyle is known as baselining. And as the young and naïve understand, baselining allows you more runway—in other words, more time—to make your dream a reality.

The runway concept is equally applicable to the more seasoned entrepreneurs with existing businesses and established lifestyles that don't lend themselves well to friends' couches or weeks of ramen. Remember our bastion of progress, David? One of his pivotal steps was to take a long hard look at his business and personal expenses and cut them where he could. Cutting his expenses down to the lowest necessary amount gave David the wiggle room he needed to bring his books strongly into the black.

Let's take a look at the elements of the runway to see how you can use it to your advantage. The equation, penned by this non-math nerd, is:

Time + Money = Runway.

Let's break it down.

Time

I don't know about you, but when I conceived the idea for my business (and the one before it and the one before that) I thought I was just about the most brilliant, intuitive, creative businessperson who ever hatched a business plan. My mad, former-secretary typing speed of 60-plus words per minute was no match for the fast flow of cutting-edge ideas pouring from my head. A 30-second elevator pitch couldn't contain me; there was just so much to say. I was white hot. Six months later I looked back on that efficiently typed business plan with disdain. A little reality showed many of my cutting-edge ideas to be more suited to the cutting-room floor. I had spent large amounts of money on ridiculous ideas, and I had much to regret. I know I'm not alone in considering my business plan to only be worthy of lining bird cages.

When traveling, conventional wisdom says to take half as many clothes and twice as much money as you anticipate you'll need. Similarly, a seasoned entrepreneur knows that every business, even the ones that get your blood flowing, will take twice as much time and twice as much money as you plan. How can that be? Robert Burns said it best: "The best laid schemes o' mice an' men / Gang aft agley." (In other words: The best laid schemes of mice and men / Often go awry.) Time gives us the opportunity to be successful. Think about your goals when you started your business. What was your revenue goal? How long did you think it would take to achieve it? (It's okay to stop for a little chuckle here.) Imagine your timeline had been set in stone and your business had a self-destruct button set for that date. Would you have been frantically trying to figure out which wire to cut, or cruising Monte Carlo in your Ferrari? I'll say it again: you'll need twice as much time and twice as much money as you think you'll need. Can I hear an *amen*?

Take "The Donald" for example. As of this writing he has filed business bankruptcy petitions four separate times.[1] When I practiced bankruptcy law full time, I used to joke that we should give him a punch card: after four he gets the fifth one free. If even The Donald, a billionaire business mogul endorsed as an expert by no less than reality TV, doesn't get it right every time, how can we mortals expect anything more of ourselves? And note that his failures resulted in bankruptcy: the white flag, the most drastic solution. You know he threw a lot of Hail Mary passes with the full strength of his fortune and influence before those petitions were filed.

Despite our brilliance, each of us needs time to identify our target market, design the product or service that will best appeal to them, market, tweak, pivot, and market some more. You can't come up with an idea, test it, and make adjustments in a few days—at least, not well. It takes time. Time is both the friend and enemy of business. We need time to refine all the elements that make us successful, but if we run out of time, what we planned to do next matters not.

As entrepreneurs without a venture capital bene-factor, we need to factor in the personal side too. Even couch-surfing ramen-noodle eaters need *some* money. The rest of us need even more. Some of us have other people like spouses, children, and older parents relying on us for support. Time is our frenemy there too. If we don't have enough time to make our business success-ful, we've not only let down ourselves, but we've also let down those who trust and rely on us.

Remember, Time + Money = Runway. So now let's look at the Benjamins.

Money

As much as we may hate to believe it, money is the lifeblood of any enterprise. Without it the enterprise comes to a halt. Have you ever seen a hungry entre-preneur? The desperation is obvious. You can smell it a mile away. My heart goes out to that frantic business owner turning over every rock to find the magic gold coin to continue on just one more day. And yet, like a desperate girl looking for a boyfriend, no one is less likely to be offered that coin.

When we're talking about money we need to con-sider both sides of your life that use money: the busi-ness and the personal. I've devoted an entire chap-ter to how to put together a strong decision-making process for business expenses in Chapter 4, so I'm going to devote this section to a discussion of personal expenses. But first, a story.

There is an old Cherokee legend about a grandfather teaching his grandson about life. "There is a fight going on inside me," the wise grandfather said to his grandson. "It is a ferocious fight between two wolves. One of the wolves is evil. He wants me to be selfish, to be angry. He wants me to be proud and consider myself first. The other wolf is good. He urges me to love, to be kind, to be generous. And I'm not alone; the fight between the two wolves going on inside me is going on inside every other person too." The grandson considered his grandfather's words for a moment and asked him, "Which wolf will win?" The old Cherokee grandfather simply replied, "The one you feed."

Likewise, there are two wolves inside every entrepreneur. On one side stands the wolf that loves to play. This wolf has worked hard for years and knows he deserves the best things in life. He has sacrificed to achieve his station in life. He is educated and experienced. All around this wolf are other wolves living in lavish caves and dining on the finest gazelle. This wolf is ever mindful of what the lesser mortals enjoy. On the other side stands a wolf that knows he must sacrifice yet again to realize a greater good. He knows that despite what he deserves, he will never get to the goal without discipline, and it doesn't matter what his comrades are doing.

Which wolf will you feed?

One of the constant realities of life as an entrepreneur is the tension between keeping money in the business and bringing it home. As much as we would like to pretend that the business exists in a vacuum and all the income it generates is available for marketing, staff, computers, software, services, and so on, that's not reality. The time and effort you're investing in building the business would otherwise be used to build someone else's business in the form of a J-O-B, and we know, for all their downfalls, J-O-Bs at least bring home the bacon. So must your business. The question is, how much bacon?

You can't keep all the money in the business. Your work in the business is a service to the business, and someone—that's you—needs to be paid to do that work. Even further, a business must be healthy enough to support its founder, even in the earlier days. The last thing you want to create is a business that needs *all* its income to continue to exist. That's not a business, that's a charity. So if we agree that the business should be throwing off some of its income to the founder— you—how do we financially savvy entrepreneurs determine what's healthy for you and the business? When you're in the process of moving away from your start-up roots to a new model of a mature business separate from you as an individual, you are going to need to err on the side of the business. Remember David: He had to fill the business's gas tank so it could grow. He had to give more to the business during the transition than it would require in the future to make that leap, to make the business efficient and profitable. In giving more to the business, David had to give less to himself. In his story, David made some pretty radical lifestyle changes. He sold his house, he sold his cars, and he gave up lobster and caviar. Now we are going to put together what those changes should look like for you. Do you need to match David's changes, engage in fewer changes, or go even further?

Your Current Financial Health

In this chapter and the next, we're going to help you get a firm grasp on all the numbers in your business and personal life. You're going to be able to put yourself in one of five categories:

1. **The picture of financial health.** You are swimming in financial awesome sauce. You own it. You work hard both as a business owner and as a person, and you are achieving success in both your business and your life.

2. **Starting to catch the sniffles.** Overall your life and business are going well, but a few nagging things must be addressed before the title of Awesome Sauce is bestowed upon you. You need a solid plan and a few pivots.

3. **Sickly.** It was the best of times, it was the worst of times—it depends on the time of day

you ask. You have a lot going for you and your business, but it's on financially shaky ground and that plagues you. It's time for some chicken soup and a good kick in the hiney.

4. **Gravely ill.** These are uncertain times. You believe in your business, and you believe in yourself, but something's not right. You need to separate the wheat from the chaff and move in the direction of all that is positive.

5. **Gasping for breath.** You are standing on a house of cards and you're waiting for it to come tumbling down. This not a fun position. You need to do some major triage and create an exit plan so you can live to fight another day.

The category in which you find yourself will determine your marching orders. It will determine the level of change you'll need to make in your personal expenditures. Just like a sickness, the sniffles might entail a day of lying in bed watching trashy TV, whereas gasping for breath will necessitate a 911 call and a crash cart. Don't mistake one for the other. You don't want to hit a fly with a hammer; a flyswatter will do much less damage to your tabletop. But you also don't want to be caught with only a flyswatter when a bear is sitting in your kitchen.

Remember that money buys many things, the most important of which is time. Time is your ally in the quest to create an amazing business that's of service to the world. Read a bit further how to put a solid number on your runway and how to play with that number to suit your goals.

A note about lifestyle design: If I know entrepreneurs the way I think I do, those of you who haven't done much reading on lifestyle design are liable to hop right over this part; more power to you. I read and listen to a lot of thought leaders in that area because, despite my love of being a mother and a wife, there's a strong wanderlust/escapist streak in me that lives vicariously through the adventures of others.

In the lifestyle design/entrepreneurial subculture there are a lot of creative ideas about getting through the start-up phase and extending your runway by baselining expenses. Some of these ideas are pretty radical. I would caution you to know yourself and really think through what's important to you as you sift through these ideas. One that's very popular among lifestyle bloggers is the idea of baselining via moving to Southeast Asia and other developing countries. This is a legitimate method of bringing your expenses as low as possible to extend your runway without actually living on a couch.

Be cautioned, however, by one who has lived the expatriate lifestyle, that there are very real tradeoffs in moving to another country and losing your bedrock of stable friends, family, and culture, not to mention reliable Internet. Investigate the realities of living in a different country, as well as the cycle of expatriate assimilation and reentry, and remember that massive changes in the fundamentals of your life may cause an overseas move to be counterproductive to your ultimate goals no matter how cheap the living is.

Find the Money Manager in You

Everything we've discussed in this chapter thus far relies on the numbers. You need numbers to figure out your runway and how much time you have to make your business a success. The numbers are:

- ⅄ The actual amount of income your business generates
- ⅄ The cost to run your business (i.e., your overhead)
- ⅄ The actual amount of money it takes you to support yourself and those who rely on you
- ⅄ Any other income you may have

The concept of the runway only works if the numbers work. If, for example, the income generated by your business is not enough to cover your business overhead, all the baselining in the world isn't going to extend your runway. You are going to have to cash-infuse your business and find another way to support yourself. How would you know that? If you're like David and most other entrepreneurs, you don't really know. You have some numbers floating around in your head, but they don't bear any resemblance to reality. You just have a vague scary feeling that you're building an unstable house of cards.

Fixing the Gas Gauge

I got my first car in 1986. It was a baby-blue hand-me-down 1974 Mercedes 240D nicknamed "Bluebird." It's not quite as glamorous as it sounds. The "D" in 240D stands for *diesel*. I had a sign in the rear window that read, "0 to 60 in 15 minutes." It got killer gas mileage and sported a double gas tank. That feature was probably fantastic when my dad drove the car in its younger years, but by the time Bluebird made its way to me, the gas gauge was broken and so was the odometer. Have you ever driven a car with a broken gas gauge *and* a broken odometer? It's impossible to tell how much gas you have left in the tank. It results in delusions of grandeur that leave you on the side of the road. It also leads to unnecessary panic attacks when searching for gas stations that carry diesel.

So it is with entrepreneurs with broken financial systems. As a gas gauge tells you how much fuel is left in the tank, your financial systems tell you how healthy your business is. You must commit to fixing the gauge; it's not an option to drive your business without one. Your business deserves it. You and your mental health deserves it.

You can't be a financially savvy entrepreneur on estimates and a chorus of "I think"s. You have to *know*. I am told that as a young star Madonna had a report of each day's income and expenses faxed to her wherever she was in the world. She kept a close eye on what came in and a tight reign on what went out. She asked questions. She gave orders. In contrast, a distressing percentage of multi-millionaire celebrities and athletes don't follow these practices, and those are the ones we read about on the front page of Yahoo news. As they say, you can't out-earn stupid.

Chapter 3 will tell you exactly how to keep your finger on the financial pulse of your business, but at this juncture, when talking about the length of your runway, you need to reconsider how you see yourself. You are your own financial manager, whether that's a hat you care to don or not. Remember those broke celebrities and athletes and let their mistakes operate as your cautionary tale. If you consider your job primarily to be acting, basketball, making widgets, or designing apps, you will be back to eating Ramen noodles with the remnants of your failed business on the ground around you. You are the Chief Financial Officer (CFO). Own it. There is so much freedom there. There is so much comfort in knowing, even if the news isn't fantastic. Not knowing and suffering the consequences is so much worse.

Exactly How Long Is Your Runway?

We've talked about what your runway is and we've emphasized the importance of using real numbers, wearing your money-manager hat, and giving your business enough room to fly. Now let's look at how to calculate exactly how long your runway is.

When we calculate our runway as a business owner, it quickly becomes apparent how intertwined our personal and business finances are. You can't discuss the runway in a business vacuum. It bears no resemblance to reality until you and the reality of your life are factored in. We've all got to eat.

Here's a sample of the runway table. Don't let it freak you out. We're going to go through it step by step, but I want you to see it first.

Business Expenses	$6,850	
Business Income	$4,350	
Business Net	-$2,500	

Personal Expenses	$4,500	
Personal Income	$2,000	
Personal Nut	-$2,500	
Total Amount Needed Monthly	$5,000	
Savings	$30,000	
Bank loan	$10,000	
Total Assets Committed	$40,000	
Total Assets / Total Amount Needed Monthly = Runway		8 months

Step 1

Your first step is to calculate your business expenses. Expenses are everything you currently pay to everyone. Again, it's not a guess. Take a look back at your accounting software. Don't have it yet? Try your bank statement. Who got paid and when? At this point, don't try to minimize any of your expenses to make the numbers look better. We're looking at what's currently happening in your business. You can make adjustments later. Be sure to include those expenses you pay monthly as well as the ones that are irregular. As an attorney, I get hit with a large malpractice-insurance bill once a year. If I didn't include a pro-rated amount in my monthly expenses, I'd get a skewed picture of the income my business throws off. Many business owners have relatively level monthly expenses, but if your business has a lot of non-monthly expenses, it might be better to look at your expenses on a yearly basis and divide by 12 months.

Don't get too bogged down in any of these numbers. If you have only ballpark figures, they will have to do.

Step 2

Now we want to assign a number to your business income. This can be tough to do because we are dreamers and optimists. We just *know* that each month will be better than the last; we will surely bring in far more revenue in the next 12 months than we did in the last 12 months! But just for this exercise, curb your enthusiasm. A runway built on optimism is not a runway that can be used effectively. We're going to be making some big decisions based on our runway calculation.

When you go to assign a number to your income, you can look back over the last 12 months of income, but that may or may not be accurate. If you've created a positive growth pattern in your business, and your income has increased steadily and there's no reason to believe you'd lose ground, it may be more accurate to use last month's figure or an average of the last three months. I caution you against using forecasted income even if you're in a strong growth pattern. It may or may not be true that your income will continue to grow at X percent monthly. Although we work for a dream of continued growth, we don't have control over it continuing, so for the purposes of your runway calculation, stick with a number you honestly believe you can count on in the future. Otherwise, it's just as your high-school math teacher said: "You're only cheating yourself." Save the forecasted income for your vision board.

Step 3

When you compare your business expenses to business income, you're going to get either a positive or negative number. This is your Business Net. A positive Business Net means your business is cash-flow positive, and a negative Business Net means it's not. That means either your business is feeding you or you're feeding it. If your Business Net is positive and your business is feeding you, good job. Go on to the next step. Let's make sure it's feeding you enough and that you're not too ravenous. If you're feeding your business, that means you need to add money to the pot to keep the business running. You need to know where that money is coming from. Is it coming from:

- A full- or part-time job
- A side hustle
- Savings
- A spouse's work
- Retirement
- Credit cards
- A loan
- Borrowing from friends/family

Know that if you're feeding your business, **you are the entrepreneur who most needs a solid runway calculation** because you're not only feeding your business, but yourself and your family as well. You need to know where that money is coming from and how long you can continue to work on your business. This is the runway personified.

Step 4

Now that you have a handle on the business side, do the same thing on the personal side: gather your expenses. Remember all the weird ones you don't pay monthly, such as insurance, car repair, vacations, entertainment, tuition, gifts, charitable contributions, taxes, and so on. Get a good handle on what it costs you, and those that rely on you, to live. That's your magic number.

Step 5

The last information-gathering step is your personal income. For many entrepreneurs, their only source of income is the money they earn in the business. That's fine, but don't use this income in this calculation. It will skew the numbers. This section is only for other sources of income.

For example, I worked as an adjunct professor for many years while I built my business. I didn't earn much, but it was a side hustle that allowed me to keep more money in the business. Some of you have a side hustle or maybe a spouse who works and improves your personal financial situation.

Step 6

Compare your personal expenses to your income. This is your Personal Nut. Unless you are a serious side hustler, this number will be negative—in other words, you need money to live on. Fair enough. We don't all get by on our good looks and sparkling personality.

Your Personal Nut is the amount you need to bring home to feed the family.

Step 7

It's time to put all the numbers together and calculate your runway. For this step, compare your Business Net to your Personal Nut (it's a tongue twister, I know). When you do so you'll see one of four scenarios:

1. Your business brings in enough to support your Personal Nut. Congratulations, you have the Qamdo Bamda* of runways. As long as the numbers don't change (but they will), it can be endless.

2. Your Personal Nut is enough to support your negative Business Net. Remember, if you have a negative Business Net, you are feeding your business. It's not common, but sometimes a Personal Nut is actually enough to make up the shortfall. We see it most in people with a serious side hustle, another existing business, or a spouse who is crushing it. Great, you're at Qamdo Bamda too, and your runway can be endless.

3. Your business brings in some of what you need to support your Personal Nut. This is the most common scenario. Go to the next step to see just how long your runway is.

4. Your Personal Nut doesn't bring in enough to support your negative Business Net. This is a critical runway situation. On to the next step to see how critical it is.

* *Qamdo Bamda Airport, in China, has the longest runway in the world, at more than 18,000 feet (for reference, a Boeing 747 only needs 8,000 feet of runway).*

You can see that in some scenarios your runway is long enough for whatever Spruce Goose you may be trying to fly. That's good news, and knowing it is also good news. But now that you know, you can't sit back in your recliner and coast. Remember, your runway is based on numbers, and if those numbers change, your runway changes. Keep a watchful eye on all the moving pieces. For example, if you have a side-hustle job that provides some income and your hours are reduced, you may need to go back and redo the calculation.

If you're in one of the two scenarios in which you need to calculate your runway, we need one more step.

Step 8

Identify the assets you have that you are willing to commit to this endeavor. Those assets are going to make up the shortfall for a period of time. Here are some of the most common assets entrepreneurs use to bootstrap their business:

- ⊿ Savings
- ⊿ Retirement
- ⊿ Credit cards
- ⊿ Mortgage
- ⊿ A business loan
- ⊿ A personal loan
- ⊿ Borrowing from friends/family
- ⊿ Investors

From where are you going to pull your cash? You need to know because your runway depends on how long you can sustain your current situation using the assets you have available to you. Figure out the source of your money and how much you have access to, and plug it in.

Step 9

The final calculation necessary for a runway is long division, but don't be scared. How long will your assets last at this burn rate? Divide the amount of money you need each month (based on your Business Net and Personal Nut) by the amount of capital you have at the ready. That gives you the number of months you can sustain this financial scenario. This is your runway.

Examples

Yikes, 9 is a lot of steps and we've used a lot of words, so let's look at a few examples to help all this make sense.

Business Expenses	$6,850	
Business Income	$4,350	
Business Net	-$2,500	
Personal Expenses	$4,500	
Personal Income	$2,000	
Personal Nut	-$2,500	
Total Amount Needed Monthly	$5,000	
Savings	$30,000	
Bank loan	$10,000	

Total Assets Committed	$40,000	
Total Assets / Total Amount Needed Monthly = Runway		8 months

Here the Business Net is negative. The business doesn't make enough to support itself and the owner can't take any money out of it. The Personal Nut is negative too. There's some money coming in on the personal side, but not enough. The entrepreneur—let's call him Steve—needs money for both the business and personal expenses. The exact number he needs is $5,000 per month. He has some savings and a bank loan that total $40,000. Therefore he has eight months until he runs out of runway.

Let's play with the numbers a bit. In this scenario, let's give Steve access to more assets. As soon as we give him $100,000 in additional committed assets, his runway jumps to 20 months. If we go back and leave everything as it is in the table, but reduce his personal expenses by $1,000, he now has a 10-month runway. It's runway-math fun!

Runway Changes

As we saw with Steve, playing with the numbers in the table changes the outcome, sometimes by a lot. We saw runways from eight to 20 months. That's a big difference. You need to know that so many outside factors are acting on this table that it's not a Crockpot, set-it-and-forget-it situation. If your office rent goes up, your runway time goes down. If you lose your side hustle, your runway time goes down. If your business income increases, your runway is extended. Yippee!

As time marches on, you need to refer back to your runway to be sure it's still accurate and you're still making decisions from an accurate vantage point. When something big changes, factor it into your runway. I suggest you review your runway every month with your financial reports (see Chapter 3). You can also put your runway together with your cash flow projection in Chapter 6. Knowing your numbers and what's happening in your business is very freeing.

Extending Your Runway

The best news about a runway is, unlike an airplane's runway in real life, you have the power to change it. You can change the numbers by changing your choices. Remember our friend David from the Introduction: He changed his choices, changed the numbers, and changed the runway.

The goal is to get to an infinite runway. Let's look at a table for inspiration.

Business Expenses	$6,850	
Business Income	$15,000	
Business Net	$8,150	
Personal Expenses	$4,500	
Personal Income	$2,000	
Personal Nut	-$2,500	
Total Amount Needed Monthly	-$5,650	
Total Assets Committed	$0	

Total Assets / Total Amount Needed Monthly = Runway	Infinite
As an added bonus, Amount Saved Monthly	$5,650

Isn't that just the most beautiful table you've ever seen? It can be yours!

Always Let Your Runway Be Your Guide

Your runway is your gas gauge. It tells you how far you can go before running out of gas. For me, running out of gas in the Bluebird meant hours spent on the side of the freeway waiting for AAA. Running out of runway in your business means the death of the business. It means the death of your dreams.

It's not enough to hope and pray. The numbers are there for the using. The numbers don't lie; in fact, they go the extra mile and let you know exactly where you stand. With that knowledge is power—power to change the outcome, power to play with the numbers. Which numbers do you have control over? Which number changes will make the biggest difference in your scenario?

You don't have to have the Qamdo Bamda of runways to be successful. The runway is there to allow you to fly. You're not expected to take off like a helicopter. This isn't the A-Team, and no vertical leaps are required. Knowing your runway and planning for it is financial savvy. Financial savvy is freedom. Remember how David's business blew up (in a good way) once he knew his numbers and stopped guessing? No entrepreneur leprechaun showed up with a pot full of gold, but yet his world changed. He morphed his runway table from something scary to something beautiful.

I've seen it time and time again. There is amazing power in knowing. Having a number, be it eight months or 20 months, lifts a burden and lights a fire. It bequeaths an incredible power of focus. You're not waiting for the other shoe to drop. You know how long you have. Your brain cells are freed up to craft and scheme. Thoughts and ideas come to a calm mind much more readily than a stressed-out and frantic one. You are able to relax when you're home rather than struggle to try and keep panic at bay. This one exercise, the exercise of knowing your runway, can change your entire business and your life.

Chapter 2:

Getting the Teenager off Your Couch

Businesses start off like babies: cute and cuddly. You'd do anything for them. You move heaven and earth to see them thrive. But at some point a business, like a baby, can become a slovenly teenager vegging on your couch eating Doritos and watching MTV all day. Your business and your teenager need boundaries. To help your business grow to adulthood, you want to slowly but surely cut the financial ties. With teenagers the ties are easy to identify, but in business, it can be tricky. Hidden ties exist and might not be uncovered until it's too late.

In addition to having your business stand on its own two feet, you want to minimize your risk as the business owner. If something were to happen to the business, you don't want it to take down your financial house of cards. You want to move away from sinking or swimming together. When your business doesn't rely on you, you are free to create wealth. When your business can still take you down, you don't have freedom. Here "The Donald" has taught us well: despite his multiple bankruptcies, he's still a high roller.

This chapter explores how the different people and entities around you view your business and its entanglement with you personally. These people and entities include:

- ⌄ The IRS
- ⌄ Your landlord
- ⌄ Your vendors
- ⌄ Your creditors

Each has a distinct legal position that views you and your business either as one or as separate entities. This is important because you need to know which assets are at risk when things go south. Ideally, it's none.

The Role of Your Entity

Whether you know it or not, you have an entity. An *entity* is defined as: A lawful or legally standing association, corporation, partnership, proprietorship, trust, or individual. Has legal capacity to (1) enter into agreements or contracts, (2) assume obligations, (3) incur and pay debts, (4) sue and be sued in its own right, and (5) be accountable for illegal activities. When you have a business, you have an entity. You can't opt out or opt in; you have one automatically. Even failure to select an entity is selecting an entity. Let me explain: An entity is the legal structure of your business. It's the framework in which it operates. Whether we like it or not, legal structures are important because they dictate both (1) tax consequences (or "benefits" if you're looking for the positive spin) and (2) liability. Those are two biggies in the business world.

Tax consequences dictate what you're paying our friend Uncle Sam. Wise vs. foolish tax choices can make a huge difference. Your entity dictates how your business is treated by the IRS. This is where your CPA is valuable. Liability is your life or death. What happens in your business either passes through to you or it doesn't. We don't want it to. Consider the classic grocery-store grape slip: There are dirtbags out there who have made careers of getting injured at retail stores. Under two of the five entity types (described next), when that dirtbag slips and falls, he has access not only

to the assets of your business, but to your personal assets as well. That means the dirtbag is cleaning our
your kids' college account, putting a lien your house,
seizing and selling your jet ski...bad, bad news. Under
three of the five entity types, our grape-tripper is able
only to move against the assets of the business. Your
personal assets are protected.

Here's a quick rundown of each of the five basic
entities, with their positive and more challenging
attributes.

1. **Sole Proprietorship.** A sole proprietorship
   is the default mode. No matter how big your
   business is or how sophisticated, if you don't
   make any proactive moves and you own the
   business alone, you'll be a sole proprietorship.
   Sole proprietorships are easy to set up and
   maintain (clearly), but provide no tax benefits
   or liability protection.

2. **Partnership.** If you're doing business with at
   least one other person, and you don't make a
   proactive move, your default mode is a partnership. The bad news is that just like a sole
   proprietorship, partnerships give you no tax or
   liability benefits. If you choose to be a partnership, you need a good Partnership Agreement
   in place for when one of you is ready to head
   in a different direction or if something untoward happens. If you do it right, you're already

doing some work, so you should look at one of the other possibilities while you're at it.

3. **Limited Liability Corporation (LLC).** These are the little darlings of this decade. Formerly they were not available in every state and the IRS parameters were a bit squiffy, but things have firmed up and LLCs are ready to roll. You'll see they're the most popular entity on the block. LLCs provide tax benefits and are more flexible than corporations. They also provide liability protection gold, and to add to their allure, they're easy to keep up.

4. **C Corporation.** The C corporation and S corporation (#5) are kissing cousins. They are formed the exact same way, but the S corporation has one more step and a few more restrictions. C corporations are the corporations people are talking about when they talk about a corporation. They're the Mac Daddy of liability protection, but they have a significant drawback in tax land by way of double taxation. Is there type of taxation worse than double taxation?? Double taxation occurs in C corporations because the corporation pays taxes, and when it distributes income to its owners (shareholders), it pays tax again. To add insult to injury, there are a lot of what we call "corporate" formalities: to avoid undoing all your good corporation work, you need

to hold meetings, keep minutes, and file certain reports with your state. We call that high maintenance.

5. **S Corporation.** God created the S corporation to keep the gold liability protection of a C corporation and avoid the double taxation. There are more limitations on which corporations can elect to be an S corporation, and the high maintenance that plagues a C corporation is also present here, but if your business meets the criteria, S corporations are great.

A full treatment of each of the entities is outside the scope of this book, and you should always consult with your business attorney and a CPA before you make a selection. I know that's a common refrain, and we all start diets and exercise programs without consulting our doctor, but for entity selection we really mean it.

Here's a quick-reference chart for you that shows you what each type of entity is good and bad at.

	Tax Benefits	Liability Protection	Easy to Set Up	Easy to Maintain
Sole Proprietorship	-	-	*	*
Partnership	-	-	*	*
LLC	*	*	-	*

C Corporation	*	*	-	-
S Corporation	*	*	-	-

KEY:

* This entity does this well

- This is a drawback to this entity

Failure to Maintain Your Entity

If you have an entity that requires formalities such as holding meetings, keeping minutes, and filing reports, failure to keep up with these formalities can undo all the good you've done by setting up your entity. It's as if your entity doesn't exist. Here's how.

There's a little-known but very real legal concept called "piercing the corporate veil." Your entity is that corporate veil because it stands between you and the business. It also could be called the corporate brick wall, but it's not as substantial as all that. This legal principle applies to C corporations, S corporations, and LLCs. Note that it's not needed for a sole proprietorship or partnership because they didn't have any liability protection to begin with. *Piercing* the corporate veil is when the court sets aside that liability protection and lets the grape-slipper reach right through the corporation and into your pocket. It's a lose-lose situation because no matter how much double tax you paid, the corporation's not going to protect you from that multi-million-dollar grape slip.

Here's what the corporate veil looks like on an elementary school playground: Imagine a bully has cornered you to take your lunch money and bloody your nose. Coming in to save the day is your tough older brother Johnny. Johnny stands between you and the bully. The bully's only left with what he can find on his side of Johnny. Then, to your horror, a bystander blurts out that last week you bent the corner of Johnny's mint condition limited edition Mighty Adventures comic book. Veins pop out on the side of Johnny's neck, and he steps aside and allows the bully to clean out your pockets. Your corporate veil has been pierced.

Just as you have to keep Johnny happy to insure your protection, you have to keep your corporation or LLC in good standing and up to date to be protected there.

Contracts Rule

If you have a C corporation, an S corporation, or an LLC, you and your entity have separate banking accounts, checks, and credit cards. You file separate tax returns. You are separate from your business in the eyes of the IRS, and this is awesome. However, despite all indications to the contrary, the IRS does not rule the world.

What we do as entrepreneurs for the great and glorious IRS won't suffice for the other people and entities we regularly do business with. IRS regulations don't govern your relationship with your landlord, your vendors, and your creditors—contracts do. You have a contract, written or oral, with everyone you deal with. Most contracts are written. They can be something you hashed out on a napkin over an Awesome Blossom, a document you drew up with an attorney, or something presented to you by the creditor itself. The content of those contracts rules the relationship and liability between the parties. The contract dictates the terms of the agreement as well as who is liable for it. If you have a contract in which you agree to be personally liable, your entity won't protect you from that liability. The agreement between you and the IRS isn't a factor in the court's eyes.

When You Are on the Hook Personally

Having an entity isn't enough to separate your business from yourself. Lots of businesses have a beautiful LLC or S corporation and are still as entangled as spaghetti. You need actual, legal separation, and that is the equivalent of getting the teenager off your couch. You've raised him and now it's time for him to fly on his own. Your business can't continue to rely on you to guarantee its contracts and debts for sustainability. It needs to stand on its own two feet. It needs to be responsible for its own life so you can live yours.

Personal liability is brutal. I can't tell you how many times I've had to explain this to someone sitting in my office; it's always a sad day because we're having the discussion after something unpleasant has already hit the fan. Once you know you have this problem, it's too late for the solution. Your personal guarantee of a business debt puts your personal assets on the table, regardless of the entity you have in place. A personal guarantee is like cosigning a loan. You've given the creditor another place to look for satisfaction—your wallet.

In Chapter 7 we'll talk about exact strategies to untangle your business and personal finances. At this point, you need to know *where* you are at risk. You need to know where you have personally guaranteed a business account, either intentionally or unintentionally. Let's look at the elements of your business and see where the personal guarantees, if any, lie.

Loans, Promissory Notes, and Lines of Credit

If your business borrows money, the business is liable for repayment. However, many lenders, both large and small, want a personal guarantee as well. They don't feel the loan is secure enough with just the business on the hook; they want the business owners on the hook too.

I've had a lot of clients who didn't know they personally guaranteed a loan until the lender came after them. That's something you need to know. Personal guarantees are the ultimate in harboring a snotty teenager. Here's how you know if you've personally guaranteed a loan:

1. On the first page of the loan documents or contract, where the parties are listed, your name is listed both as the representative of your business (for example, Emily Chase Smith, President of Awesome Yogurt, Inc.) and individually (for example, Emily Chase Smith). Your name showing up there twice says you're signing in two capacities: as representative of the business and as yourself. The second one is the personal guarantee.

2. You are asked to sign the last page of the loan documents or contract twice. This again will be as the representative of the business and as yourself individually.

3. A paragraph in the loan documents or contract discusses a "personal guarantee" or "personal liability."

You can go back through your loan documents and see if you've signed only in your representative capacity or if you've personally guaranteed the loan as well. If you *have* personally guaranteed a loan, and if your business defaults on it for whatever reason, the lender will pursue you as well as the business. Just like Susan, you'll be personally named in the lawsuit, and your personal assets will be on the line.

Contracts

As a business owner, you enter into contracts for many different things. Generally these contracts are between the business and a vendor. Some vendors may slip in or even outright require a personal guarantee. It's less common than for loans or leases, but it happens. To see if you're personally liable, look for the same things in a contract that you would in a loan document.

Leases

Commercial locations, automobiles, equipment, software, and other leases follow the same rules as loans. Your lease may be limited to the business only or it may also involve a personal guarantee. You'll look for the same things in a lease that you would in a loan or contract.

Note: Don't trust anyone but yourself to make this determination. If you're unsure, speak to a local lawyer. I had a client who asked her friend who was also her real estate broker this exact question and he assured her that she was not signing as an individual, only as the owner of the business. Unfortunately, the real estate broker was wrong and she discovered it when she was sued personally. This is your business and your life. Be sure the person you trust is in the position to know.

Credit Cards

This is a tricky one because the vast majority of small business credit cards are personally guaranteed even if the card has only the business name on it. In fact, even credit cards issued to large multinational companies and given to their employees for business expenses such as travel have been known to contain personal guarantees. Yikes.

The key here is your cardholder agreement. It's the contract between you and the credit card company. But guess who drafted it and who it benefits? Nine times out of 10, there's a personal guarantee in there. It's tough to get a solid answer on whether your credit card has you personally on the line. You can call the company, but you can't rely on what the $10/hour representative on the line tells you. You're best served to assume that you've personally guaranteed all of your business credit cards even if you haven't doubly signed the agreement.

To add another layer of complication, business credit cards are generally not reported on your personal credit report even if they are personally guaranteed. In fact, they are only reported if they become delinquent. So a look at your credit report isn't going to flush out these personal guarantees.

Collateral or Secured Items

This is not a personal guarantee per se, but it acts a lot like one. This is a situation in which a loan is secured against an asset you own personally. The Small Business Administration (SBA) is notorious for requiring collateral for their loans. This means they will lend you $100,000, but they will require an asset to secure it against, such as a piece of real property—in other words, your home. If you default on the loan, they can take the property. That means you as an individual are supporting the business via this type of loan.

Untangle the Money Spaghetti

Financially savvy entrepreneurs understand that although the entanglement of personal guarantees may be necessary to start the business, the sooner the business is financially independent, the better. While you are personally responsible for the business, your personal fortune is at risk. Selecting and maintaining the proper entity will give you positive tax treatment and protect you from liability, and recognizing and eliminating your personal guarantees will allow you to hold your own purse strings.

Chapter 3:
The Numbers Game

If you've ever gone in search of financial help you've noticed that a lot of what we hear in personal finance, we as entrepreneurs just can't use. It makes no sense for us to make a lovely color-coded spreadsheet of all our income and expenses with a nice, stable salary number up top. We wouldn't even know where to start—the colors, maybe? We require something more, something flexible that takes into account all the moving pieces.

In fact, because of those moving pieces, it's even more important for us to have our finger on our financial pulse than those with a traditional J-O-B. Remember Bluebird, that stylish 1974 Mercedes with the broken gas gauge and odometer? If that were a garden-variety employed person, when it ran out of gas, a tow truck would be along in 30 minutes—that's the next paycheck. It's coming; it's just a matter of waiting. As entrepreneurs, we're hoofing it to the nearest gas station, finding a gas can, pumping it full, and carrying it back to fill our car ourselves. You can see how vital it is that we entrepreneurs don't strand ourselves in the middle of the Mohave.

I'm a huge fan of the reality show *Shark Tank*, in which aspiring entrepreneurs pitch their ideas to a panel of potential investors (sharks). I find it to be an easy, entertaining way to introduce my kids to entrepreneurship (except my 5-year-old, who is only interested if what's being pitched has wheels). One of the sharks, Daymond John, is a self-made multi-millionaire, the founder and CEO of FUBU, and an investor. I read an interview with him on Entrepreneur.com and just about fell out of my seat. In it, Daymond said,

"While good business ideas are plentiful, many entrepreneurs struggle to understand payroll taxes, healthcare, and other thorny issues.... In other words, they don't have the financial literacy to scale their businesses and attract investors."[1]

Daymond John is looking into my soul and preaching my sermon for me. Amen, Daymond. Yes, business ideas, execution, and hustle are all important, but lack of financial savvy will kill your business every time. You see this in lotto winners: 44 percent have spent their multi-million-dollar winnings within five years. Why? Because income alone does not guarantee financial savvy.[2]

Knowing Your Numbers

As a bankruptcy attorney, my favorite clients to work with are business owners. They are smart people, and they tend to move rather than spend a lot of time thinking or delaying. They are really a joy to work with and I often wish we were meeting under different circumstances so we could go get a cup of Joe and talk business rather than file a bankruptcy. But throughout the years I've noticed a common denominator in my clients: they don't have a handle on their numbers. In the bankruptcy arena, numbers are king. As attorneys we need to tell the story of the past, present, and future with numbers—numbers we can support with proof. As I start the numbers discussion with clients, so starts the hemming and hawing. Very few have a profit and loss statement generated from an accounting software system. Almost no one comes in with a spreadsheet containing the financials of the business. I'm much more likely to see a shoebox with receipts and invoices or a plastic grocery store bag with un-opened envelopes. That's the dump of whatever was on the desk and floor of their office.

Which came first, the sloppy accounting or the fi-nancial distress? It's a chicken-and-egg question, but I know from sitting across from many, many business owners that the ones most likely to end up in my office don't know what's going on in their business finan-cially and haven't for a long time (if ever). Remember, these are good people. These are hustlers who often have had successful businesses that supported them for years. But these are also the people who don't really know what's going on in their business and are shoot-ing from the hip in making business decisions.

I've talked about established entrepreneurs, people who have been running businesses for many years, and often many decades. What about the newbies—those just beginning to spread their entrepreneurial wings? How important is financial savvy to them? Can they make the mistakes of all start-ups and clean up later? Let me start with an example.

My brother played baseball from about the age of 7. Now, our family has some pretty strong genes: all the men are tall and thin. We'd never be picked first for anything requiring brawn. As a result, when young we tend to resemble malnourished gazelle. I distinctly re-member my stick-thin, knobby-kneed brother walking onto the baseball field for the first time. I can't imag-ine the coach thought, "Here comes my star." It was probably more like, "I hope that kid doesn't faint on me. Get him some lunch." But did that coach treat my Bambi brother any differently than the beefier, more muscular kids? Nope. He planned on success for all of them. He coached all of them as if they were the ones who would eventually give him World Series tickets behind home plate.

It's the same for your Bambi business. It looks leggy and malnourished now, but plan for success. Don't put it out in right field and forget about it. Give it coaching. Show it how to hold a bat. Give it lunch. All the financial principles are just as valid for the newbie as they are for those who have been in the game for a long time. That skinny buck may be your big ticket.

If we are to know what's happening in our business, we need some numbers. Please don't let your eyes glaze over here, and don't get up to get a bowl of ice cream. I am going to make this as simple and painless as possible. You're not an accountant and I don't want to make you into one, but this is the foundation of financial savvy.

Let's say you found out that providing a certain service to a client took five hours and brought you $1,000, but providing another type of service took three hours and brought $1,500. Which client would you want to clone? What if you discovered that you spent $5,000 in products, but by the time you factored in your overhead, you made only $100. Would that be a product you want to put a lot of thought and effort into? Having solid numbers like these and knowing what's in those numbers will allow you to guide your business to your most profitable products and services. Here's how it gets done.

Setting up Your Books

You need an accounting system. Some people effectively use a simple spreadsheet or notebook during their early months, but this method lacks the ability to generate reports. It's just a fancy checkbook for your business, and it doesn't tell you much, if anything. You want the ability to look at your data in a meaningful way. The newer you are, the more important that can be because you have less margin for error. Move to a proper accounting software as soon as possible. It's not as expensive or complicated as you may fear; accounting software is much more cost effective and simple to use than it was in the past. I'll give you a few recommendations here.

There are three leading accounting software solutions: Quickbooks, Freshbooks, and Less Accounting. Many more are available, and it's much more important to pick one and use it consistently than to choose any particular one. All three I'm about to discuss are Cloud-based, so you (and your bookkeeper) can access them remotely.

1. **QuickBooks.** QuickBooks is the industry leader. It's the PC of accounting software. You can't go wrong with QuickBooks. It will give you every report you can imagine and then some. It will grow with you. You can run your multi-million-dollar company using QuickBooks. The downside is, because it was first, it's a bit clunky and not always intuitive. It's also the most costly of the three, but it's still pretty reasonably priced. It will handle business.

2. **Freshbooks.** I like Freshbooks more and more every day. It's cost effective and easy to use. It even looks cool. Freshbooks also does time-based billing very well. In fact, that was its original purpose. If you bill clients based on time spent, Freshbooks makes that easy.

3. **Less Accounting.** Less Accounting is the Mac of the online accounting world. It's cool, it's hip, and it's super intuitive. It's set up to be an alternative to everything people hated about QuickBooks. If you plan on doing your accounting yourself, this is the way to go.

All in all, picking an accounting system is a toilet paper argument: under or over, it's all personal preference, and the important thing is that you use it. All three of the systems I mentioned have a free trial period, so you can try them all and choose your favorite.

Again, just be sure not to let the analysis paralyze you. Pick one and use it.

Keeping Your Books

Once you've selected your accounting software, the next question is, who's going to be using it day to day? Many business owners hear the word "bookkeeper" and equate it with "out of my budget." It sounds expensive, but I advocate a bookkeeper being your first hire. The financial awareness they bring to your business is worth their cost, and it likely doesn't cost as much as you think.

If you're considering being your own bookkeeper, I'm here to talk you out of it. Consider:

- **Your accounting savvy.** Do you have any experience in keeping books, perhaps your personal books or in a former job? Are you familiar with accounting principles? Do you know how to generate and read reports? If not, do you want to be your own guinea pig?

- **Your tech savvy.** How easily do you learn new software and systems? How much patience do you have? Will this take time away from your higher business functions?

- **Your need for accountability.** Are you a self-starter on projects you don't find exciting? Do you do better with someone else on your team holding you accountable by waiting for your information or input? Having a bookkeeper on board will assure the information is put in and that useful reports are generated.

Here's why hiring a bookkeeper rocks:

⋏ She has the accounting knowledge. There are no questions about whether something is done right. It's right.

⋏ She knows the accounting program and how to use it. No one is wasting hours trying to figure something out.

⋏ No longer is there a fear of shoebox creep— that information will be opened and out of the shoebox because your bookkeeper needs it to do her job.

When you're new, small, or working within a tight financial scenario every decision has a big impact. You can't afford as many mistakes. It's like driving on a freeway that's under construction: To your left is a concrete barrier, not an emergency lane. Any small deviation from the course can be fatal. Hiring a bookkeeper, especially if you're solo, can be daunting. It sounds expensive. If you don't have a ton of money flowing in and out of your business you can wonder if you are able to afford one. I'm here to tell you you can.

After I went off to college and my younger brother and sister were off doing their teenage thing, my mother decided to fill in the family pool rather than do the full rehab it needed. But you don't just fill in a pool, especially in landside-prone California. You need to seriously break up the concrete to allow for drainage so you don't come home one day and find your house down at the bottom of the hill. Then you need to fill it with clean, compacted dirt. To break up the concrete, my mom rented a jackhammer. I should take a moment to remind you that my family is not an especially physical people. We can weed and dig sprinkler trenches, but use of a jackhammer was not in our repertoire. I couldn't even hold the thing, let alone use it. One day I came by the house and saw my brother sweating down in the deep end of the empty pool, attempting to make some headway with the jackhammer while not cutting off his foot. As I watched him labor away, I asked my mom what it would cost to have a professional fill in the pool.

Now, my mom is thrifty. Some would say *cheap*, but she prefers *thrifty* (love ya Mom). It hadn't occurred to her to get a bid on filling in the pool; she presumed it would be cheaper to do it herself—and using a jackhammer is one of the few benefits of having a teenage boy. Well, after a few phone calls, she returned the jackhammer, called off the backhoe, and my brother sat leisurely sipping lemonade as the professionals did the work more cheaply than she could. The moral of the story is that doing it yourself isn't always cheaper, and you may lose a foot.

The great news about bookkeepers is you don't need a lot of their time. They are fast and they know the program so just a few hours a month will keep your books shiny and clean. The other great news is that a lot of traditionally employed bookkeepers love side work. It's easy money for them to do just a little more of what they do all day. You might find a bookkeeper you'd love to work with among people you already know. For example, I hired my bookkeeper from the last law firm I worked for. I knew her, liked her, and most importantly trusted her. She did the accounting for a large 20-plus lawyer firm with multiple locations so I knew she could handle whatever I threw at her.

The very best part of hiring a bookkeeper is that it frees you up to work on your business. Are you more valuable as a marketer, networker, or writer, or as someone who inputs checks, client payments, and expenses? Give yourself permission to do what you set out to do—build a business.

Let me pause here and make a note about selecting your bookkeeper among your family. You might be thinking, "My Aunt Freda is a bookkeeper; she'd be great and she'd probably do it for free." Time for a heretical statement: Free is bad. You want someone who is invested in your business, not just doing the work when there's nothing on TV. You *want* to pay for this. Have you ever had a friend or colleague tell you that he knows there's something majorly wrong on his Website and he's waiting on his buddy (who did the site for free) to fix it? Yep, the cobbler's children have no shoes. You don't want to be waiting for your reports to see the state of your business, but *Dancing With the Stars* is on and so you wait. Pay for bookkeeping.

Also, when you put family and finances together things can get weird. Aunt Freda knows exactly what you're bringing in. If it's significant, you can bet she's not going to be doing the books for free for very long. And when it comes time to pay her, it's probably going to be a premium, because how can you lowball such a special aunt who put in all that free work? You see where I'm going with this? That freebee is going to cost you dearly.

Categorizing Your Expenses

One of the most important places you and your bookkeeper can spend your time (I did talk you into that, didn't I?) is categorizing expenses. This will allow you to see exactly what's giving you the most mileage in your business, to see what's most profitable.

Let's say you build gorgeous custom furniture including kitchen tables you ship all over the country. To market your kitchen tables you have special pictures taken of them set with fancy dinnerware and yummy food. Let's say you even bring in some beautiful people to act as models, having a grand time around your table. You also buy a piece of software for your Website that allows customers to put together their dream table and see exactly what it would look like in their home. All this costs a pretty penny. Beautiful people are not cheap.

Before you hire the first beautiful person, you e-mail your bookkeeper and ask her to set up a "kitchen table" category. As the invoices for your extravagant spending come in, the bookkeeper marks them "kitchen table." So many come in that you begin to abbreviate to KT. For a few months that KT category is looking scary. The expenses are piling up and even the dog is getting nervous. But after those few months you notice that the number of orders for kitchen tables appears to be rising. In fact, it feels as though you're building four times more kitchen tables than anything else. As you sit down to review your financial report you see that in fact you have recouped your extravagant expenses and then some in just three months. As you review your reports monthly going forward you watch the KT category begin to shine like a beacon. This tells you a few things:

1. Your decision to go all-out in marketing kitchen tables online was a great idea.

2. The money spent in the KT category will continue to bring in new kitchen table customers for years. You've spent the money once, but it continues to drive business.

3. The tickle in the back of your mind about doing something similar with bookcases is likely a great idea.

Because of your financial savvy, you now know more than 95 percent of your custom-furniture competitors. You make more than what you're good at making or what you like to make, but what makes you money. Win!

Mining for P&L Gold

Your profit and loss statement (P&L), also known as an Income Statement or Statement of Operations, is like California in the mid-1800s: there's gold in them thar' hills, and your job is to get it out. Your P&L can drive your business. Let's call it mining for P&L gold.

If you're new to the gold rush, I recommend dedicating an hour a week to pore over your profits and losses. Just one hour a week will change the way you run your business. Instead of driving in downtown Los Angeles without a map trying to find great Mexican food, you'll be armed with Yelp and Google Maps, making your goal much harder to miss. You won't be guessing at how to run your business, you'll have a strategy.

Once you've spent a few months communing with your P&L on a weekly basis, you can shift to monthly. But once there's a big decision to be made or you feel you might be on shaky ground, weekly reviews will once again become your BFF.

Here's my review system. It takes just an hour (either weekly or monthly) and is designed to find all the

P&L gold and turn it into actionable steps you can take in your business. Set a timer for each step to make sure you're not cheating yourself and your business of five or 10 minutes. You need to give your great brain time to work its magic.

1. **Review: 10 minutes.** Take the first 10 minutes to familiarize yourself with your expense categories and what you're spending on them. This is your first look at what's been happening in the last week or month.

2. **Circle: 10 minutes.** Take a pen to it and circle anything that stands out. What numbers pique your interest? Does something appear to be larger or smaller than expected? Is something different from your last review?

3. **Ponder: 20 minutes.** Oooh, this one's hard. Put the P&L aside and sit quietly for 20 whole minutes and let your great brain process what you've seen. Let it run wild. Let it make connections. Let it ask questions. It's especially important to give yourself the full 20 minutes. Think about romantic dating: When did you really learn something about the other person? Was it in the first few minutes, or was it later when you had time and space to listen and process?

4. **Review #2: 10 minutes.** Pick up your P&L again. Now that you've pondered, what do you want to know? What numbers do you want to

review? What new expense categories do you want to create?

5. **Notes: 10 minutes.** Now you finally get to pick up the pen and turn your brain waves into activity. This is where entrepreneurs shine. As yourself:

- ▲ What is working?
- ▲ What do you want to change?
- ▲ What further information do you want?
- ▲ Whom do you need to talk to?

This is your action list. This is where the numbers speak to you. This is where you take what's working and what's not and make the necessary pivots. This is the P&L gold. Lay down your picks and shovels, because you've found it.

▲ ▲ ▲

Financially savvy entrepreneurs have their finger on the financial pulse of the business. If you do what's recommended in this chapter, you will too. These few systems will make a world of difference in your business. You won't be guessing anymore. You'll know.

Chapter 4:

What's Eating Your Lunch?

Money comes in, money goes out. There's an ebb and flow we're familiar with as business owners, and it's comfortable. We know you need to spend money to make money. That's been true since our lemonade-stand days. Without lemons, cups, and an actual stand, there's no business.

Let's take a little quiz. Nod your head if you've ever:

- Made a dumb marketing decision. I recently threw away more than a thousand postcards left over from a campaign that didn't work out. Not only was the campaign a waste, but I had bought the materials in bulk so I had a lasting reminder.

⅄ Hired or kept on a staff person you didn't really need because (a) she was related to you; (b) he did one or two valuable things with his time, but not much, or (c) the idea of firing her made you nauseous.

⅄ Rented too much space thinking you'd "grow into it."

We've all made dumb money decisions in our business. Some are tragic and some require an extra-large trash can (I'm looking at you, ridiculous number of postcards). We are always going to make dumb decisions; there's no way to avoid them. We just want to be sure that they don't shock the system or even kill our entire business.

6 Dumb Decisions

In this chapter we'll explore how to minimize the number and impact of dumb decisions. This will give you a framework from which to make wise business decisions that will keep more money in your pocket. Let's start with the six most common:

1. Saying, "It's a write-off"
2. Not controlling business expenses

3. Losing perspective
4. Going large
5. Getting the office *and* the car
6. Indulging in too many luxuries

1. Saying, "It's a Write-Off"

Coupled with our zest and creative entrepreneurial ideas there's a major mental factor working against us as we make financial decisions in business: the deduction. Do any of these scenarios sound familiar?

- You're deciding between buying a new delivery truck and a used one. You stop by the car lot. As you're asking questions the salesperson says, "It's a write-off" with a wave of his hand, and you drive off the lot in a new one.

- You inquire about new inventory-tracking software. As you get into the discussion of cost, there it is again—"It's a write-off."

- You're standing in Best Buy deciding on a new cell phone for your business and you don't even need the sales guy to tell you, "It's a write-off." It's Pavlovian, you've already told yourself.

"It's a write-off" is the justification we use to buy something we want. It's the same as "It's on sale." It stops the true analysis of how that item will serve us and whether the cost makes sense in our business. "It's a write-off" takes the sting out because there are no real numbers involved and it makes everything sound like a bargain.

2. Not Controlling Business Expenses

Business expenses are often incurred without being carefully considered. No matter what your business, you will benefit from keeping a tight rein on the money because **money only counts if you keep it**.

Would you rather have:

- A business that brings in $10 million a year, with expenses of $15 million?

- A business that brings in $1 million a year with expenses of $500,000?

Clearly, you're feeding the first business and the second business is feeding you.

This discussion always brings to mind M.C. Hammer. No matter your position on parachute pants, by any measure, in the 1990s M.C. was rocking it. Forbes put his net worth at $33 million. He had hit records and we were all singing "U Can't Touch This." So how, a mere five years later, did he file bankruptcy, listing $13 million in debt?[1] It's the classic "$33 million in, $46 million out." My guess is there was just a teeny bit of unwise spending there.

3. Losing Perspective

My dad is an architect. When I was young he built houses and churches. Later he moved to shopping malls and schools. Think about his day: He's building, and working the numbers for these huge projects. At that point, what does a $100 lunch mean? That's less than the doorstops for the science classrooms. Money gets skewed when it flows in large volume. Its value gets distorted.

As entrepreneurs we command enough money monthly to pay for our costs, the business overhead, our staff's salary, our salary, and, if we're doing it right, profit. That's a lot of money flowing into and through our business and our hands. We might be forgiven for not being clear on the value of a dollar, but it won't serve us well.

4. Going Large

Along with the general tendency to overspend and our slightly skewed perspective, we entrepreneurs have another bit of brain junk with which to contend: We're dreamers. We're big thinkers. We see the vision and strive to create it. The end result is in full Technicolor in our mind. That mindset is both a blessing and a curse. As we run toward the goal, we act as if the finish line is already a reality instead of scaling as we grow. I'm as guilty of this as anyone.

For example, if we're building a tech company, we know we're going to be the next Google. We ask ourselves, *What does Google have?* Top talent, generous benefits, and a killer office. *What do we need?* The same!

In truth—and we know it in our hearts—is that we need to allow our business to grow. We need to allow it to be a small acorn headed toward being a mighty oak. We need to grow and evolve as the business grows, and only buy and commit to what we need right now and for the short foreseeable future, not for a year or two down the road. Paying for items month after month that aren't necessary means you aren't able to afford the things that could really make a difference in your business. You might not even consider other things because you're too busy trying to pay for what you already have. Let's look at an example.

You have a beautiful office, filled only halfway because you're going to "grow into it." It's in a great location and nicely appointed—and expensive. It's about twice as much as you'd be able to get away with. Let's say the office costs $8,000 a month and you could have rented something in the $4,000 range that would serve your current purposes. A few observations:

1. You are able to bring home $4,000 less every month right off the bat. Money spent is the same as money not earned. The extra $4,000 that could be profit is being used to pay the

rent when could be doing something else, like lining your personal pocket.

2. You are missing $4,000 in other opportunities. Is there a marketing campaign that would build your business? Is there software you'd love to implement that would improve workflow and cut staffing costs? Those things aren't going to happen because that money is already being used on empty space.

3. You are setting yourself up for a $4,000 struggle each and every month for the term of the office lease. Let's say you signed a three-year lease; that's 36 straight months you need to come up with $8,000—when it could have been $4,000. That's an extra $144,000 throughout the term of the lease. If you suffer a downturn or things get tight, that's not a cost you can cut.

I'm you, so I know what's going on in your mind right now. You're saying to yourself,

"But we're growing. We'll need that space before three years passes. What are we going to do when the office gets too small? Move? That's a hassle. We're really just planning ahead."

Here's where I want you to trust yourself. You're an entrepreneur, and the thing entrepreneurs do best is solve problems. When you need the space, the space will appear, Grasshopper. You'll creatively solve the problem of where to put people as you grow. Businesses move all the time. In the meantime you'll have the cash you need to grow.

The office example is an easy one to hang onto. Use it as a comparison case to buy or commit only to what you need right now. Dream big, but commit only to today.

5. Getting the Office *and* the Car

Sometimes it's hard to know where to spend for the business—everything appears important and there's always a salesperson there to tell you why you just have to have this particular thing. Here's a framework you can use when the decisions are harder than the size of an office space: Put yourself and the item you are contemplating in the realtor/lawyer and office/car category. Realtors need nice cars because they drive clients around to view property. Lawyers need nice offices because that's where they meet with clients. Realtors like nice offices and lawyers like nice cars, but they don't *need* them. This comparison is easy to do when it's someone else, right? Notice the common factor: the client. What is the client experiencing? What is the end result for the user? Spend on what your clients will see now, and grow into the other, less important items. Here are some examples:

Profession	Office	Car	Other
Lawyer	Thumbs up	Thumbs down	Stellar furniture
Realtor	Thumbs down	Thumbs up	Quality signs and design
Tech company	Thumbs down	Thumbs down	Customer service system
Trainer	Thumbs down	Thumbs down	Great wardrobe
Ice cream shop	Thumbs down	Thumbs down	Amazing customer space
Dry cleaner	Thumbs down	Thumbs down	Great POS system

Interestingly, it's easier to see the forest despite the trees when you look at an industry other than your own, because you are the consumer/client there and not the business owner. You know what you see, therefore you know what's important and what's just fluff.

Now, before you think I'm just advocating the business version of "cut out the morning latte," know that I love nice things. I mean, I *love* them. In my business, I *need* a great computer. I *need* a great Website and good podcasting equipment. I *need* really nice business cards and a really nice purse and laptop bag. I *don't* need a nice car or a nice office, because most of my clients are remote. They don't know where I'm sitting or what it looks like. It took me a while to figure this out. I'm a lawyer by profession so I assumed I needed a nice office. I went ahead and rented and furnished one, and I used it at first, but as my business grew and evolved I realized I didn't need it. The turning point was when I landed a big client who lived in my city, but I never met him in person. We didn't need to meet. We did all our interacting on the phone and via e-mail and fax. I spent the summer I worked for that client in Costa Rica. He never knew. It didn't matter. I came back and let my office lease expire because clearly I didn't need it. Now I work from my home, and as I type this, my view is of rooftops, palm trees, and blue ocean. I'm sitting on a couch with a blanket keeping me toasty—and I'm bringing home more cash.

On the other hand, I do a lot of speaking and traveling. I can't show up with a ratty purse and laptop bag looking like I haven't gone shopping since 1984. I need to look the part of a successful speaker, not a salesman on the road stretching his last buck. So even though shopping for clothes is not my thing, I spend money there because it creates the customer experience.

This is not about me being a killjoy, telling you to drive junky cars and work in crummy offices. It's about you making choices that will drive your business to success (see how we did that?).

6. Indulging in Too Many Luxuries

A financially savvy entrepreneur knows there is a time and a place for luxuries. Luxuries are one of the reasons to be an entrepreneur. If we wanted just an "okay" living, we could get a J-O-B and uncomplicate our lives. Luxuries are good. They are fun. God made Mercedes for a reason. But if luxuries are impeding your cash flow you end up with a garage full of Mercedes, an empty fridge, and a dead business.

The Big Decisions: a Framework

Many moons ago I worked for a large law firm that represented mobile home park owners in California. It's an incredibly niche market—our clients were the companies that own the land, utilities, clubhouse, and pool that make up a mobile home park. California has a specific section of the Civil Code devoted to the interaction among mobile home park owners, the residents, and those that lend money for the residents to purchase a mobile home. I worked where the park and the residents interacted, solving resident issues.

I enjoyed the work because it was never dull—something funky was always going on in a mobile home park somewhere in California. There were the angry neighbor fights in which one resident saved up his personal waste to put on his neighbor's lawn, and the erstwhile entrepreneur who met the junior-high bus with pages from pornographic magazines to trade for cigarettes. Crazy pet issues, substance abuse...it all went down at the mobile home parks; there was never a dull moment. I called it my Jerry Springer job. So the work was interesting, but it involved a lot of court work all over the state. In case you're not familiar, California is *big*. Trials are almost always scheduled for first thing in the morning, and often I'd have a five-hour drive coupled with an 8:30 a.m. trial call. I experienced a different kind of wake-up call one day when I was in court getting a restraining order to keep a particularly violent resident away from a scared park manager while we evicted him. The resident wasn't present at the hearing, but as we left the courtroom, we met him in the hall. True to character he stepped up to physically intimidate the diminutive female park manager. As I threw my nine-months pregnant body between them, the light bulb went on. This is what I'd chosen for my life: keeping truck driver's hours, dragging my trousers all over the state, and putting myself in harm's way. I'd made an initial choice to work in this field and I was making a daily choice to stay there. It wasn't long until I transitioned out and into something less potentially deadly that let me sleep until after the rooster crowed.

> *The doors we open and close each day*
> *decide the lives we live.*
> —Flora Whittemore

Life and business are a series of decisions. You frequently stand at a crossroads and wonder which is the best way to go. Have you ever seen another business owner make a decision and head down a path, and you thought, *Why the heck did he do that?* Maybe you later talked to him about it, and he said something like:

- ⅄ It was the pressure of the moment.
- ⅄ I didn't have enough information.
- ⅄ I didn't have the right information.
- ⅄ I just wanted to make a decision and move on.
- ⅄ I don't know what I was thinking—it seemed like a good idea at the time.

You make ton of decisions in your business, both large and small. In fact, one of the definitions of an entrepreneur could be "decision-maker." Each decision you make directly affects your business and your life. Here are just a few examples of decisions you could face in a short period of time, and what kinds of questions you need to ask yourself before you decide.

- ⅄ **Decision:** To take or not take an investment from a particular source

     Questions to ask: Is this person or firm going to be an asset, or micromanage me into an early grave? Is it enough money? Is it too much? What are we going to do with it? Do we have to pay it back? If so, how will we do it?

⅄ **Decision:** Whether to begin production on a new product

Questions to ask: Is this going to be a big seller? How is it different from what's currently on the market? Can we handle the initial costs? How will we position it? How will we sell and distribute it?

⅄ **Decision:** How to brand your messaging and your business

Questions to ask: Who's going to help us with this? What needs to be done? Does what we're considering represent us well? Will it speak to our target audience? Is it cost-effective?

⅄ **Decision:** How to handle a disgruntled customer

Questions to ask: What is his complaint? Is it legitimate? Who is this person and how wide an impact does he have? Do we need to make internal adjustments to fix an issue based on this complaint? How can we make this customer satisfied?

⅄ **Decision:** Whether a particular staff member is working out

Questions to ask: Is she a good fit with the other staff? Is her job performance adequate? Can we improve it? Does she have the core skills and attitude necessary to be great?

Do we have the resources to bring her up to speed?

You don't want to jump into making any one of these decisions lightly. They are all complicated issues with many moving pieces. If you have a framework and process, you won't be guessing and hoping, you'll a reasoned decision based on the information available. You'll remove as many of the wild cards as possible. You can have confidence in your decisions. There's a simple 3-step process that will revolutionize the way you make decisions. It will remove the knee-jerk approach to decision-making and will give you confidence in the decisions you make. Here's how it works.

1. Set the date.
2. Brainstorm.
3. Consult the Party of 3.

Step 1: Set the Date

Many people begin the decision-making process with brainstorming or information-gathering. They jump in with both feet, wanting a quick resolution, but they're missing the first, and most important, step: to ask yourself, *By what date or time does this decision need to be made?* The first step is *always* to consider the time frame in which the decision needs to be made, because the longer you can take to make a decision, the better one you can make.

You'll notice in competition TV shows there's always an element of time—and it's never quite enough time. Take *Project Runway*: you have one day to create an unconventional look from pet products. And *Top Chef*: you have 30 minutes to take gas-station ingredients and create a masterpiece. Time matters, and the faster you're required to do something important, the more likely you are to screw it up. Great for reality TV, terrible for real-life business. Science supports this idea. A study by Veronika Grimm and Friederike Mengel of Maastricht University School of Business and Economics looked at the effect delaying decision-making had on the wisdom of the decision. They used the Ultimatum Game, in which player A offers a portion of $10 to player B. It can be any portion he decides. If B accepts A's offer, both parties get the amounts. If B refuses A's offer, both parties receive nothing. Low offers, of, say $1 or $2, are almost always rejected, even though, from player B's perspective, $1 or $2 is better than no dollars.[2]

In Grimm and Mengel's study, they introduced one element: a questionnaire. Now, this questionnaire had nothing to do with offers, lowball or otherwise. Its purpose was solely to delay the decision of player B, to interject some time between A's lowball offer and B's decision. The study showed that player Bs who made a decision immediately after receiving a $1 offer always rejected it, but if player Bs took 10 minutes to fill out a questionnaire after receiving the lowball offer, acceptances went up to 75 percent. That's a *huge* jump in acceptance. We make better choices if we take a pause.

So the first step in the decision-making process should always be to ask yourself, *When does this decision need to be made?* One way to make that determination is to ask when your risk profile will change. At what point will the sand shift beneath your feet and you won't have the same buffet of choices? Let's look at our examples again.

⅄ **Decision:** To take or not take an investment from a particular source

   Time determination: To determine when the risk profile would change you could ask yourself how long the offer is likely to be open. Perhaps the investor has given you a week to decide—there's the date. The offer won't be available after that date.

⅄ **Decision:** Whether to begin production on a new product

   Time determination: When will the pricing you've been quoted change? Is the product seasonal? When does production need to begin? When is the financing available and when does it dry up?

⅄ **Decision:** How to brand your messaging and your business

   Time determination: Is there a particular event you're running or attending? Is there a season in which you are trying to capture attention? When is the designer/consultant available? Are there any discounts available by working in a particular time frame?

⅄ **Decision:** How to handle a disgruntled customer

Time determination: Where is the customer? Standing in front of you, or online? What is the issue, and how quickly could it be resolved?

⅄ **Decision:** Whether a particular staff member is working out

Time determination: How timely is the work he performs? How potentially serious are the issues? Can you use him in a different capacity while you determine his suitability?

As you can see, determining when the risk profile will shift is a decision in itself.

▲ ▲ ▲

Now you have a baseline idea of what time frame you have to make a decision. It's important to use *all* your available time, because additional options may open themselves up while you're deciding. Things change, and giving yourself the risk profile timeline gives things that opportunity. It's the same reason you never walk into a house you're considering buying and start gushing about how "perfect" it is: If you do that, you never know what options in terms of price might make themselves available. Knowing how much time you have to make your decision also gives you time to gather information and consult trusted advisors. Bottom line: extra time that doesn't change your risk profile is always a good thing.

The other thing the risk profile analysis does is set an actual date. That means, even if the timeline is relatively long, it's still a timeline. The decision will still be made by you, and not by default. Because you've set a date, the decision won't be allowed to make itself and potentially cut off great options for your business.

A caveat: some decisions don't really have a clear date by which the risk profile will change. The example of rebranding is one. So if you're facing a decision on which there's no strong date, pick the date by which you want to have moved on. Give yourself enough time to make a good decision and balance that with the desire to move on. Move outside the question mark. Fish or cut bait.

Step 2: Brainstorm

Once you've set your decision date, it's time to let your "great brain" work on the problem. What do I mean by that? Well, to bring you up to speed I have to tell you a short story. My favorite set of books as a child was The Great Brain series written by John Dennis Fitzgerald. The Great Brain was modeled on the author's older brother, Tom Fitzgerald, and the series was set in turn-of-the-century Wild West Utah. In the series, The Great Brain is always using his superior thinking to either swindle his siblings or solve an important problem for the community. Although he's only an elementary-school boy, he knows the power of his Great Brain and will often go into the barn and "let his great brain work on it." Now, a hundred years later and no matter where you live, I'm asking you to go into the proverbial barn and let your great brain work on the issue.

Set a timer. Pick an amount of time, and let your mind run free for the duration, just as you do weekly with your P&L. Committing some time to a decision that will have a big impact on your business and your life is a good investment. For this pondering time, get out of the office. None of your best, most creative ideas came while sitting at your desk, did they? Get outside, get moving, and get those juices flowing.

While you're brainstorming, think about:

- What's your first thought or gut reaction? Your first instinct isn't always the answer, but it can provide the baseline for your future thinking.

- What's the easiest thing to do? What's the path of least resistance? Sometimes the simplest answer is the best. Other times it's a cop-out. Which one is it here?

- What data are you using and where did the data come from? Is it from your business, from your books? Is it from someone trying to sell you something? Do you need other data? Can you get it in the time frame? From where?

⅄ What's the worst-case scenario, and how likely is that to happen? If it did happen, could you live with it? Is this an "all in" move? Is that what you want?

⅄ Have you made a similar decision in the past? What was the outcome? How is this decision different or the same?

Let your mind wander and be creative. Let your Great Brain loose.

Step 3: Consult the Party of 3

Any big decision deserves more than one Great Brain. After you've set the decision date and let your mind wander, it's time for the roundtable. Pick three people whom you respect and reach out to them for a five-minute phone call or a one-question e-mail. Pick people whom you think have experience in the decision you're making. You want to tap into that experience and find out what you don't know, what you're not experienced enough to have considered.

When you reach out, be very clear about the parameters. It's a one-question e-mail or a short phone call. Be respectful of the time frame and be the one to

cut it off and thank the person for her time and wisdom. Be sure to use the word wisdom—people love
that, and it's true. They have wisdom where you don't.
Don't belabor the discussion, because you want to be
able to tap her again if necessary.

In addition to tapping a wealth of information,
when you ask other people for their wisdom, you've put
your issue and options into words. You are able to ar-
ticulate the issue and the potential solutions. You might
find some clarity comes in just asking the question.

Step 3.5: Calendar a Review Date

As a final step, put a date on the calendar to review
the decision. Pick a date far enough away that you'll
have some perspective on how it all worked out. You're
not looking to re-make the decision later, but you also
don't want to fix it now and forget it. You want to use
your experience to step up your decision-making in the
future. When you take five minutes to look back on a
decision you've made, you'll gain a lot of wisdom.

Final Notes on Decision-Making

Not deciding is also a decision. If the President
leaves a bill long enough on his desk without signing or
vetoing it, the decision makes itself; the bill is law. You
operate under the same principles. If you don't decide,

you've decided. You've taken control out of your hands and given it to someone else. Not your finest moment.

If you find that you have to talk yourself into something, it's usually a bad decision. Good decisions aren't effortless, but if you're performing backflips to justify it, it's probably not wise. Look into your motivation. It may be that you're trying to please someone or do someone a favor, and it just doesn't fit. If it's a big struggle, look elsewhere for your solution.

If you find yourself paralyzed, it's likely due to the Paradox of Choice. This is a large, complex theory, but one part of it says that when too many choices are on offer, we get paralyzed. Think of your kids in the cereal aisle—total overload. One way to combat the Paradox of Choice is to narrow your options down (perhaps artificially) to just three or four and use those as your base. Even if you've eliminated a potentially good choice, you've moved the train farther down the track.

My final thought on decision-making is to have confidence in that you earned your place as the decision-maker. No one handed you the keys to the kingdom. You worked for them; you earned them. You are the one making the decision because you've built your business to the point where this decision is even possible. You are able to start a new marketing campaign or product. You have customers with the potential to be disgruntled. Own your decisions. Have confidence in your decisions because you're the one person in the world uniquely situated to make them.

Chapter 5:

The Most Important Business Plan You'll Ever Draft: The Exit Plan

I recently read Jim Collins's book *Great by Choice*. As are all Jim's books, it's fantastic, filled with wise words backed by years of research. In this book Jim delves into how the most successful companies have survived in turbulent times. He uses the story of the 1996 Mount Everest disaster as an illustration (the subject of the book *Into Thin Air* by Jon Krakauer). That year, an experienced guide, Rob Hall, led a group of people bound for the top of Everest. It's a long, arduous, costly journey to reach the summit. In every such group, on each day in which they make their bid for the summit, a time is set by which the party must stop their movement forward, turn around, and head back for camp. We'll call it the turn-around time.

Turn-around time is pivotal when climbing Everest. The leader has to ensure the party has enough daylight, strength, and oxygen to get back to the safety of the last camp. But turning back means not reaching the summit, something the leader has promised and the expedition participants have planned and trained for, sometimes for years. In short, when the turn-around time has passed, the expedition has failed. Based on the conditions, the turn-around time for Rob Hall's 1996 group was 2 p.m. For many "good reasons" and despite years of experience, Hall decided to extend the turn-around time past 2 p.m. That decision, coupled with other events and circumstances, cost him his life and the lives of seven others on the mountain.

It's a tragic story that illustrates an important point: Climbers on Mount Everest set a turn-around time. SCUBA divers clock the oxygen left in their tanks. Road-trippers monitor the gas gauge, anticipating the next fill-up. When darkness descends at the local park, you pack the kids into the minivan and head home. Unsurprisingly, this same concept applies to your business. You need a turn-around time. You need to quantify the cost before you're on the mountain straining for the summit and every "good reason" keep you moving forward, and you never make it home.

Mount Everest climbers turn around. SCUBA divers come up for air. Road-trippers stop at the next gas station. Mothers call, "Kickstands up!" They're all exit plans. Exit plans keep climbers and divers alive, road-trippers on the road, and kids out of the park after dark. In business, exit plans allow you to:

- Stay out of the bankruptcy court
- Open another business
- Keep your family relations intact
- Retain retirement funds
- Have somewhere to live and something to eat

You live to fight another day. The time to make the decision about when to turn back is not when you're caught up in the excitement or anxiety of attempting to summit a mountain, it's at the base of the mountain, before you take the first step. The time to make the decision on how much time, money, and effort to spend to make a business successful is not when you're in the driver's seat, totally immersed in the daily decisions. It's before you even launch. That's not cynical, it's wise.

The Exit Plan

Most business owners put together some type of business plan before launching their business—some even commit it to writing. The business plan covers the concept, location, customer base, competition, financial requirements, and more. As important as that business plan is, it only addresses one thing: the business. And it only addresses one conclusion: success. The plan presumes you'll reach the summit.

As true entrepreneurs we know that this is our current and most favorite business, but not our last. Our minds are a hive of buzzing creative activity. We've had business ideas and businesses before. This is the one we fancy now, but we're not hanging up our boxing gloves if it doesn't succeed. We are more than the success or failure of this one business, and we want to outlive its conclusion.

In addition to being serial entrepreneurs, another characteristic is in play: We are hustlers. We make things happen. We leave no stone unturned, and that serves us well in our business. However, in our earnestness to make our business dreams a reality, we pull out all the stops. We take it to the wall. In our zest, we fail to plan for a downturn or outright failure. No one wants to talk about failure at the beginning of a business—it's like frostbite discussions at the beginning of an Arctic trek. It feels like jinxing the plans. But failure to plan for something that could be a reality leaves your fingers and toes at risk and your life on the line.

Going into any new business without an exit plan is a dangerous proposition, but fortunately the solution is very simple. A well thought-out, written exit plan will, as we said in law school, CYA, or *cover your analysis*. An exit plan sets down exactly how much money, time, and effort you are going to commit to the success of the business. It details the exact turn-around time. It's not a difficult document to create, and it can be your lifeline.

Interestingly, anecdotal stories suggest your chances of success will increase when the boundaries are clearly marked. It's not hard to see how that might be the case. When you know exactly how much money, time, and effort you have at your disposal, you tend to make better decisions. These are finite resources, and an exit plan is a constant reminder of their limits. With your exit plan in place, you can throw all your creativity, passion, and time into your business. You won't waste precious energy lying awake at night worried about money or resources because you know exactly what you've got. The difficult decisions have been made. You've got a plan.

Remember Susan from the Introduction? Susan had a business that was a slowly sinking ship, but she didn't know that at the time. Susan poured her best into the business—all her best ideas, contacts, time, and energy. Of course, along with all her personal best, Susan also poured all her money. First it was savings. Then she used all her available credit. Before long, Susan had used her retirement. Note that I didn't say *some of* her retirement; she cleaned out her retirement account, little by little.

By the time Susan came to see me, she was deeply in debt, with a huge tax bill for pulling retirement funds out early, no employment prospects on the horizon, and creditors hounding her at every turn. They called while she was in my office—true story. The bad news I had to deliver is that whereas I could help her get rid of debt and the lawsuit, I couldn't create income, restore retirement accounts, or handle most tax issues in bankruptcy. The damage had been done. Some damage was reversible and some wasn't. I still had to send Susan from my office destitute, wondering how to feed her family.

Susan's not dumb. She's incredibly smart, but she didn't have an exit plan. She didn't have a turn-around point. She didn't leave any gas in the tank for herself and her family. Susan rode the train all the way into the wall.

How to Make Your Exit Plan

An exit plan is an internal "for your eyes only" document that marks the exits. It's like what you see on the back of a hotel door: It's for use only in emergencies, to execute your safe exit in the event something untoward happens. It sets out in clear numbers where you draw the line in your pursuit of this particular business.

Take a generic 8 1/2-by-11 piece of paper and divide it into three horizontal sections. Label them:

Time

Money

Effort

Each of these three sections represents a stopping point, or exit, at which you leave the business. These are the turn-around points. If you hit any one of these, you are going to stop this business and begin the next adventure. This is stopping the train before it hits the wall.

Time

Under Time, you are looking for a date representing exactly how long you will work at this venture to make it successful. This is a drop-dead date. As you choose this date, remember what an exit plan isn't: It isn't a manifestation plan or attraction thinking. It's not there to motivate you. Think back to the 2 p.m. turn-around time for summiting Mount Everest. That is the absolute last minute you want to still be on the mountain—it gives you the longest amount of time to reach your goal while leaving you enough oxygen and stamina to get back to camp. That's what you want here.

Be expansive in your thinking. Give yourself some latitude. You want to hit a sweet spot that gives you time to make your business a success, but keeps you from laboring for years at something that's not working. Have you ever known someone with stars in his eyes? He's going to be the next big thing? It's painful to watch him continue to try and win that spokesmodel spot on *Star Search* when it becomes more and more clear with every passing year that it's not in the cards.

There are no right answers, just a right time frame for you and your business. The time frame you select will reflect opportunity cost. In other words, while you're running this business, you're *not* doing something else or pursuing another million-dollar idea. How much time are you willing to invest in this one dream?

Money

The second criterion is money. How far are you willing to go financially to make this business successful? Remember Susan. A business is like a spoiled teenager: it will take any and all money you're willing to throw at it. The question for this section is, where is the line?

There are several categories of money available for businesses, and I've divided them into two sections, **Money to Use for the Business** and **Money Not to Use for the Business**. These sections represent two sides of the same coin. You, as the business owner, are generally the one funding the business. In this portion of the exit plan, you'll decide what money or available credit you plan to use for the business. On the other side, you'll decide what specifically you are going to leave in reserve for your family and your next venture.

There are several forms of **Money to Use for the Business**. They could be:

⅄ **Savings or investments.** How much are you willing to use from savings or investments you already possess? This is a dollar figure. What's that number?

⅄ **Credit, loans, and credit cards.** How far into debt are you willing to go for the business? This is the stickiest one. It's so easy to take on debt in many forms without actually looking at what you're borrowing. How much debt are you willing to hold?

⅄ **Home equity.** This is a subset of debt, but I treat it differently because it has different ramifications. Most debt can be cleared up by bankruptcy or negotiation, but a loan against your home generally can't. When you mortgage or take a second loan on your home or the home of a relative, it's a risky proposition. If your business fails, grandma loses her house to foreclosure. I've seen it happen. It's brutal. This is the place to say whether that risk is part of your plan.

Money Not to Use for the Business looks a little different. You're looking to assign a number to:

⅄ An amount of savings or liquid funds you will retain for yourself

⅄ Retirement funds you will not invest into the business

Note that I didn't include an amount of credit you are going to keep available. Sometimes people look at the money turn-around point that way. They figure they'll just be sure they have some available credit on credit cards to bridge them through tough times. But credit dries up; the tap is turned on and off at the will of the bank. Keeping available credit isn't part of an exit plan because it may not be there when you need it. In fact, if you really do need it, it likely won't be there.

Effort

The third section isn't financially related, but it deserves a place in a plan for when to turn around. For those of us with families, the kind that rely on us, business is not only a numbers and money play. It's not a win to finish with a wildly successful business if our marriage or our children are in shambles. The effort section of the exit plan gives you and your loved ones assurance that you will not choose the business over those things that are most important to you.

This section fluctuates based on who you are and who is counting on you. It's more challenging to determine than the other two. Here are some examples of what you might want to include as your turn-around point.

⅄ If my marriage is suffering

⅄ If my children are distant

⅄ If I am disconnected from what is going on inside my family

⅄ If one of my children requires more attention due to a personal crisis

Note that a lot of these items can be fixed without closing your business, but they are going to require a huge rethink about how you are working your business. They're going to require a conscious effort and a big shift.

This section of your exit plan is baking into your business an awareness of what's going on in your family as you build your business. It's a sad thing to contemplate, being a successful entrepreneur who lost your spouse and children. If you wouldn't take a check for $10 million in exchange for your family right now, today, don't inadvertently create the same situation.

Putting Your Exit Plan in Play

You know why an exit plan is important. You know the elements and what goes into each one. Now here's what to do with your fancy-schmancy exit plan:

⅄ Make it official. You know what that looks like to you. Type it up. Put it in a plastic sleeve. Decorate it with colorful stickers.

⋏ Put it somewhere important.

This document represents the substance of your commitment to yourself when you're not in the thick of things. It's like deciding how many M&M's you're going to eat before you sit down with the bag.

An exit plan is not something you're going to look at on a weekly or even monthly basis. It's your commitment to yourself in writing. It's the fire-escape plan on back of hotel door. You know it's there and you know when it's time for a gander.

Chapter 6:
Keep the Cash a-Flowin'

I love a good road trip. You never know what you're going to discover with the miles and days stretched out before you. So let's pretend the best-case-scenario lands in your lap: You get a letter from a lawyer in New York on fancy stationery telling you an uncle you never knew has passed away and you are the sole heir. This uncle was loaded. Seriously loaded. You have untold millions waiting for you in New York. All you have to do is show up in person and claim it. It's road-trip time!

You load up the car and head out from your home in California. Nevada, Utah, and Colorado go well, but as you hit Nebraska you start to get nervous. Your wallet is light and you fear you might not have enough money to get to New York. As you pull into Iowa, your worst fears are realized. You're broke, standing at a gas station in Des Moines in a full panic. So close to millions, and yet so far. If you can't get a cash infusion, and fast, you're stuck in Iowa with no prospect of getting to New York.

Such is your business. If you can't make the journey, you can't claim the reward. Businesses fail for many reasons, but one event guarantees failure: running out of money. The fancy term is *undercapitalized*, but the result is the same.

How Much and When

In our road-trip example, we were heading to New York not just for holiday, but to collect a large inheritance. The issue we faced at the gas station in Des Moines wasn't really the lack of money—plenty of money was on the horizon. The issue was having money *at the right time*.

I'm writing this chapter sitting at the mall while my daughter is engaging in the teenage ritual of shopping. Although it's mid-November, you'd think Santa was going to arrive any minute. Retailers make so much of their money during the holiday season, and that money has to last through the times when the teenagers are playing sports or laying out at the beach rather than shopping. It doesn't matter that the busy season is on the horizon. If a retail shop owner runs out of money in July, the shop won't be around to help us stuff the stockings in November. It's not only a matter of how much, but of when.

Projecting Cash Flow

By now I'm sure you suspect I'm secretly (or not so secretly) trying to turn every reader of this book into an über money-nerd. *"Projecting cash flow"? That sounds complicated.* Not so, I protest! I want to give you just what you need to be financially savvy; no more and no less.

> *Everything should be made as simple as possible, but not simpler.*
> —Albert Einstein

Let's add a few facts to our road-trip scenario. Let's say you knew it was going to be tough for you to get from California to New York. You were so on top of things that you even knew it would be around Iowa that you'd run out of money. But you were determined to get to New York, to the big payday. So before you left California, you lined up a loan: enough to get you from

Iowa the rest of the way to New York. All of a sudden, your trip looks different. It's not a scary, white-knuckle expedition, a rage against the empty gas tank; it's a relaxing, scenic drive. Projecting cash flow makes that same shift in piloting your business.

The Spreadsheet

The term *spreadsheet* can strike fear into many hearts. It conjures up the image of hours of head-banging frustration with little to show for it. As a business owner, you are certainly not required to be able to create a complex spreadsheet from scratch, but I know you're smart enough to be able to plug numbers into cells and let Excel do all the math. That's how we're going to work our cash-flow projection: a simple spreadsheet that already knows all the formulas, and you can just plug and play.

The point of this spreadsheet is to ensure you're going to have enough cash to pay your expenses, your staff, and yourself each and every month for the next 12 months. Can you imagine the peace of mind that will bring? If not, take a moment and picture it. Each and every month for the next 12 months you will know your business is stable. You can focus on the business rather than worry about the money. You'll never be stuck at a gas station in Iowa.

Let's dive in and I'll show you how it works.

Take a look at the spreadsheet on pages 144 and 145. This will give you an idea of what it looks like. The downloadable, plug-and-play version can be found at [WEBSITE]. That's the one you want. Go download it now and we can play with it together.

On the upper right you can choose a start date. You can start this spreadsheet at any time, not just the first of the year, and it will run for 12 months. When you put the year and month in the cell, it will automatically fill in the month and year for each of the 12 months. Pretty cool, huh?

The first thing that stands out is the separation between the cash-in and the cash-out sections—and that's what cash flow is all about (sung to the tune of "Hokey Pokey").

The first line is called "Cash on Hand." That's money you already have. The only cell you need to fill in here is the first one, under "Starting Cash." That's the amount of cash you have right now. Don't worry about the other Cash on Hand cells for the individual months. I'll tell you how those work in a minute.

Next, we're going to start filling in numbers. This is the crux of the cash-flow projection; our reasonable guess as to what's going to happen throughout the next 12 months that will help us plan our money. A few notes on choosing numbers:

⮝ This is a cash-flow plan, not a vision board or manifestation thinking. Each of these numbers is an accurate, educated guess.

Year Begins: Jan-15

	Starting cash	Jan-15	Feb-15	Mar-15	Apr-15	May-15	Jun-15	Jul-15	Aug-15	Sep-15	Oct-15	Nov-15	Dec-15	Total
Cash on Hand (beginning of month)		0	0	0	0	0	0	0	0	0	0	0	0	0
CASH IN														
Sales														
Cash Infusions														
Collections														
TOTAL CASH IN	0	0	0	0	0	0	0	0	0	0	0	0	0	0
Total Cash Available (cash in plus cash on hand)	0	0	0	0	0	0	0	0	0	0	0	0	0	0
CASH OUT														
Gross wages (other than owner)														
Payroll expenses (taxes, etc.)														
Contractors														
Supplies														
Advertising														
Transportation														
Rent														
Repairs & maintenance														
Insurance														

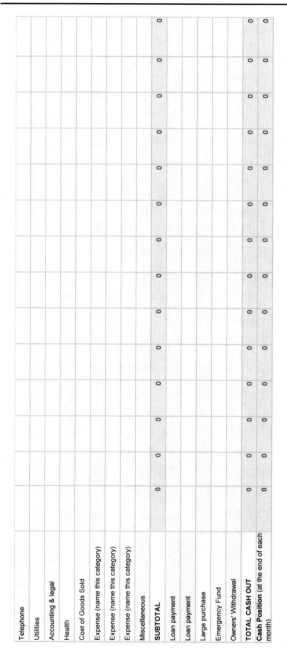

Telephone											
Utilities											
Accounting & legal											
Health											
Cost of Goods Sold											
Expense (name this category)											
Expense (name this category)											
Expense (name this category)											
Miscellaneous											
SUBTOTAL	0	0	0	0	0	0	0	0	0	0	0
Loan payment											
Loan payment											
Large purchase											
Emergency Fund											
Owners' Withdrawal											
TOTAL CASH OUT	0	0	0	0	0	0	0	0	0	0	0
Cash Position (at the end of each month)	0	0	0	0	0	0	0	0	0	0	0

I like to say realistic with a smidge of optimism.

- ⅄ If you have seen a growth in your business year to year and you anticipate it will continue, include that growth in these numbers.

- ⅄ Be sure to include seasons and cycles in your numbers. You know how your business ebbs and flows. Include it here.

- ⅄ If your business is new, you won't have any old numbers as a starting point. Take your best, educated, reasonable guess.

- ⅄ If you haven't had your finger on the financial pulse of your business, you may only have previous tax numbers available. Use what you can.

Let's start slotting in numbers and see what we get. Right under the Cash In line, you'll see three categories: Sales, Cash Infusions, and Collections. This is where you're going to anticipate your Cash In for each of the next 12 months. Put the money in the month you are going to receive it and according to its category. I'm going to say it again because it's so important: put the money in the month you're going to receive it, not when you earned it.

"Sales" includes all the money you receive from goods sold or services offered. "Cash Infusions" are savings, loans, venture capital, angel capital, and so on. It's the money that comes in other than what you've earned as a business. "Collections" is included for those who hold income on their books (in other words, they don't get paid right away). It's not common for many businesses, but it's helpful to break out the money that's been earned long ago and paid just this month.

Remember, these are all gross numbers. This is Cash In. Don't worry about expenses in this section; we'll have a spot for each one of those in the next section, Cash Out. At this point, don't try to make any numbers work. Just go with what you know or reasonably expect will happen. Don't add extra into the Cash Infusions section because you think you'll need it. We'll get to working the numbers, what they mean, and strategies in a few. For now, just put in what is already scheduled to happen.

On to the Cash Out section. This one has many more categories, but really it's just there to tease out all the expenses in your business. Don't let the number of categories overwhelm you; they're just there to keep it everything straight and make the spreadsheet usable for decision-making. These are your expenses and when you have to pay them. I've included the most common categories on the left. You may want to change the labels to reflect where you spend your money. If you don't need as many categories as I've provided, don't remove any lines, because it will wreak havoc on the formulas we have in place. It doesn't hurt to leave a cell blank or insert a zero.

Here are the categories I've included:

- **Gross wages.** This is the total amount all of your employees cost each month. Do not include what you pay yourself, even if you pay yourself as an employee. That's in another section.

- **Payroll expense.** This is the total of all other costs related to your employees, including taxes.

- **Contractors.** Here's the spot for everyone who works for the business that you pay as an independent contractor.

- **Supplies, Advertising, Transportation, Rent, Repairs & Maintenance, Insurance, Telephone, Utilities, Accounting & Legal, Health.** For each of these sections, include a number. Some may be level: for example, you pay the same amount of rent each month. Others may be less than monthly, such as Insurance and Accounting & Legal. Include the expense on the month you will pay for it.

- **Cost of Goods Sold.** If you want to break out the costs directly attributable to producing a product, you can put it here.

- **Expenses [name category].** These you can name to suit your particular business, or leave blank.

- **Miscellaneous.** There's always a miscellaneous category, but try not to use it too much—that's just lazy accounting. You want to know where the money is going, so sticking a big number into Miscellaneous is not going to serve you well.

Note: You're not doing anyone any favors by running personal expenses through your business. It might feel clever or sly, but you're causing two major problems. The first is that you're running afoul of the IRS. Don't mess with them. They have all the power. The second is that you're skewing the profitability of the business. How can you attract capital or sell the business if it looks like it's not making money? Keep business and personal expenses separate. Play straight—it's a lot less to remember and a lot less to bite you in the patootie later.

The Cash Out expense will automatically subtotal at the bottom. Under the Subtotal line, we have a few items that are still Cash Out, but we've chosen to keep and track separately.

There are two Loan payment sections. This is where you track what is going out toward loans each month. If you plan to put additional money toward a particular loan, it will go in the month you schedule. We keep loan payments separate so you can see the impact of the loan payments on your cash flow. When we get to Chapter 7 and start discussing how to best use money to make your business healthy, we will use this section of your Cash Flow Projection.

Under Loan payments is a line to schedule in large purchases. For example, if you want to buy a new piece of equipment, new software, or even launch a big marketing campaign, the amount you plan to spend in a particular month will go here.

An Emergency Fund is next. This is where you schedule an amount to set aside each month to build an emergency fund. Just as you keep cash on hand for when things to bump in the night personally, an emergency fund for your business will help you get through the unexpected. Sometimes business owners rely on lines of credit or available credit on credit cards as an emergency fund, but as we've mentioned, those have a way of drying up in a crisis. Building up an emergency fund will bring yet another level of certainty to your business and life.

The final number you need to slot in is an Owner's Withdrawal amount. This is the amount you pay yourself each month. I encourage you to select a level number: pay yourself the way you pay your staff or the way you were paid back when you had a J-O-B. Pick a number that will be consistent throughout the next 12 months, even if it's a low number. There are a few reasons for this:

1. It brings certainty to your own financial life. You can plan on the personal side how to budget your money and what you're working with each month.

2. As the owner, you are working in the company. The work you do represents value to the company. If you don't pay yourself a fair salary for the value you bring, you're skewing the company's numbers. You don't know the profitability of the company until you pay everyone who works there a fair wage, including yourself.

3. Your accountant wants you to. Check with her to be sure, but I bet she does. For tax purposes many entities require you pay yourself a market wage.

When you pick the level amount, keep in mind it can be changed as the 12 months march along. If you find you're killing it, you can adjust upward. We just want to be sure you're not using the business as your personal piggy bank. You want a real, legit business whereby you keep enough money in the business to keep it growing while paying everyone who works there a living wage.

Directly under the Owner's Withdrawal is the total Cash Out, and under Cash Out is the whole reason we engage in cash-flow projections—the Cash Position at the end of each month.

Let's pause for a minute and look at a few more logistics before we get to the exciting bit. The Cash Position is the difference between the total Cash In and the total Cash Out. It's either a positive number (there is money left over) or a negative number (there's not enough money to get through that month). The Cash Out number for each month is going to travel to the top of the next month to the Cash on Hand, whether it's positive or negative. For example, if you have $3,000 left over at the end of March, it will appear as Cash on Hand in April and will be worked into April's numbers. If you are $1,000 short for the month of March, it will appear as a negative number in Cash on Hand in April and you'll need to cover the shortfall in April.

Congratulations, you're done! Your 12-month cash-flow projection is complete. Let's get to the good stuff: what it tells you.

Your New Best Friend

Your cash-flow projection is your new BFF because it will tell you exactly where you're covered and where you're not—and a good friend will tell you the truth, not just what you want to hear.

If you start by looking at the bottom line for each month, the Cash Position, you'll see which months are projected to be your best. You can also see if you're covered for all months. If you are, congratulations. You're the winner of the cash-flow projection lottery. You can take your pretty cash-flow projection and carry on with your entrepreneurial life with confidence. You know you're covered for the next 12 months.

Alas, many of us did not win the cash-flow projection lottery. Our cash-flow projection contains some tough months. Some months are looking downright scary. Do not fear. No, you're not in lottery-ville, but all is not lost. In fact, it was more important for you to do this exercise than anyone else because you've been given a tornado warning. Now, I'm from Southern California, and what I know about tornados will not fill *Sharknado 2* with dialog, but I've seen *The Wizard of Oz* and I know that a warning will go a long way toward survival, whether you're in a farmhouse in Kansas or a mobile-home park in Louisiana. If you know the storm is coming, you have time to prepare, to batten down the hatches, as they say.

You may remember that you were the one who put all the numbers in the cash-flow projection. Those numbers are all changeable at your will. That means you can batten down your financial hatches by determining how you're going to approach the tough months. Are you going to:

- ⅄ Launch a new product sooner?
- ⅄ Delay a big spend?
- ⅄ Change your payroll?
- ⅄ Adjust your Owner's Withdrawal?
- ⅄ Find or provide a cash infusion?

Play with the numbers now, before the storm hits. Using your cash-flow projection, you know exactly what you need and when. Work to cover the shortfalls before they happen. The great news is that once you cover the shortfalls, you're in the same position as the cash-flow projection lottery winners. Your numbers match up. You too have enough money for the next 12 months. You can now carry on with your entrepreneurial life with confidence as well.

Chapter 7:
Untangling the Money Spaghetti

It's only Chapter 7, but you've already come so far on your financially savvy journey. We've journeyed through reports and keeping your finger on the financial pulse of the business. We've talked about how to make wise financial decisions, put an exit plan in place, and project cash flow. You're well on your way to being a financial rock star.

Harken back to Chapter 2 when we talked about who is holding your purse strings. We looked at different types of liabilities you may have in your business:

⅄ Loans, promissory notes, and lines of credit

⅄ Contracts

⅄ Leases

⅄ Credit cards

⅄ Collateral or secured items

Remember the key? It was personal liability. That's what caught our friend Susan. It was that sticky personal liability that took down her house of cards.

To really understand why personal liability is such a beast, it's easiest to look at it from the creditor's perspective. The creditor is the other person or company in the equation: the holder of the lease or contract, or the issuer of the credit card. When things are going well, everything moves along without a hitch. When something changes, creditors get nervous. That "something" could be:

⅄ A change in your ability to make the payments

⅄ An internal change in creditor's guidelines

⅄ A change in the health of the creditor's business

⅄ A change in the overall economy

⅄ A change in the health of your business

⅄ A change in the amount of debt your or your
company holds

Sometimes a change can make a creditor squirrelly
for no clear, identifiable reason. We don't always know;
creditors be crazy. Once a change happens, creditors
start looking at their options. Their options are guided
by their written (and to some extent oral) agreements
with you. Fortunately for them, they drafted the documents, and their lawyers are no fools. Those lawyers
planned for all the eventualities and gave their clients,
the creditors, maximum room to maneuver.

The first thing that happens when creditors get
nervous is that any existing credit is turned off. We saw
this a lot in the 2008 downturn. HELOCs (home equity lines of credit) with remaining available credit were
unceremoniously cut off. Those with plans for that
available credit had to look elsewhere. As they soon
discovered, once one creditor cuts you off, the others
aren't generally standing in line to offer credit either.
After the credit is cut off, if the contract contains an
acceleration clause, the creditor may call the entire
amount due. This routinely happens if you miss a payment. Quickly you owe not just the missed payments,
but the whole balance. That gets scary. If you can pay,
fine; no harm, no foul. You write a check. If you can't
pay, the creditor looks to collection. Collection can be
informal, such as phone calls and letters. It can also
move to litigation, a.k.a. a lawsuit. This is where the
creditor sues you to get a judgment the creditor—let's

go ahead and call this creditor "they," to simplify things—can use to collect against any assets. The key here is who they are going to name in the lawsuit: It's going to be the company *and* anyone else who is on the hook for the debt—in other words, everyone who guaranteed it.

As a practical matter, the creditor names everyone they can and they choose who they are going to pursue based on who they think they can collect from. Whom do you think is more attractive, a business that may or may not have assets, or a living, breathing person who likely has some assets? Because you owe the money, the court will generally issue the judgment. With a personal guarantee in place that judgment will be against both the company and you personally.

It's different from state to state, but in California a judgment from a lawsuit is good for 10 years and is renewable for successive 10-year terms. It can follow you to the grave. Remember, they're pursuing not only the business, but you personally. That can look like:

- A wage garnishment/attachment
- A lien on real property
- Seizing and selling real or personal property
- An assignment order that directs a third person to pay money owed to you directly to the creditor, most often seen with tax refunds and annuities

To add insult to injury, a creditor also has the right to conduct a Debtor Examination, in which you appear in court and give them all the information they need to make your life miserable, such as asset and bank account information. The judgment will also appear on your credit. This is not a good scene.

> **Note:** If an item is secured (for example, a car or real property), the creditor can foreclose or repossess the item and in many cases get what's called a deficiency judgment. This is the difference between what you owed and what they got when they sold the repossessed item. Just taking the item is often not the end of the story. You can still end up with a big yucky judgment.

Let's Keep This From Happening

Okay, this creditor enforcement stuff is not fun and I'm sorry to put the fear of God into you, but an ounce of fear can produce a pound of prevention. Let's look at how to keep this from happening. Let's flush out those personal guarantees and get rid of them.

Step One: The Spaghetti Table

Step one is to identify where you are personally on the hook for the business. Remember, we're going to make sure your business doesn't end up a smelly, Dorito-eating, MTV-watching teenager on your couch. We want your little bird to fly, so let's identify where he's codependent.

Make a quick Excel spreadsheet or Word document, or even pull out a college-ruled notebook page, and make a list of the liabilities of the business that carry a personal guarantee. We'll call it the Spaghetti Table because this is where you and your business are all bound up together. See Chapter 2 for a refresher on how to determine if a personal guarantee is in place.

The easiest way to put together the Spaghetti Table is to look at from where you pulled the money to start the business, from where you pulled money in the lean months, and whom you pay on a regular basis. You'll find clues in the Cash Flow Projection as well. You're looking for:

- Loans, promissory notes, and lines of credit
- Contracts
- Leases
- Credit cards
- Collateral or secured items

You want to ferret out each and every one of them and create a complete list. For each one, you want to notate the amount of debt, the monthly payment amount, and the terms. Here's an example to get you started.

Spaghetti Table			
Obligation	Outstanding Amount	Monthly Payment	Terms
Second Mortgage on Home	$30,000	$260	Interest only. Balloon 2/2020
Office Lease	[Number of months left multiplied by the monthly payment]	$3,500	Lease runs until 12/2016
2010 Ford F150	$8,000	$450	5%, paid off 10/15
Bank of America Credit Card	$11,000	$110	0% interest until 8/14 then 28%
Loan from Uncle Mortimer	$10,000	n/a	Pay back when we can
Outstanding Balance at Lumber-O-Rama	$5,000	$500	No interest. Pay $500 until paid off

The Spaghetti Table represents a pretty common scenario in which money has been pulled from several sources to start up and run the business. Each of the items in this table represents a place in the structure of the business that makes the owner vulnerable. Each of these items, if it can't be paid, could turn into the ugly lawsuit, judgment, and collection scenario we looked at earlier.

Note that each of the elements I asked you collect is important. You want to know the amount that's outstanding because that's what it's going to take to pay it off. You want to know what it costs you monthly because that cuts into your cash flow. You want to know the terms because they show how an obligation can change (see the balloon payment due on the second mortgage in 2020). All the elements are important for step two, The Untangling Plan.

Step Two: The Untangling Plan

If you and your business are all tied up like a plate full of spaghetti, you want that to change. You want the business to stand on its own two feet, not supported by your financial risk-taking. Ideally, that plate of spaghetti could be untangled in an evening. Realistically, it's going to take some time. You and your business didn't become intertwined in a day and you won't be separated that quickly either. The Untangling Plan will take into account the specific elements of each liability and put together a plan to shift that liability, in time, entirely to the business. At the end of the Untangling Plan, you and your business will be completely separate. You will no longer sink or swim together. You will be free to amass wealth without the fear of losing it all to a struggling business. You could shut down or sell the business with nothing more required.

Just like untangling a plate of spaghetti, it's going to take some thinking to untangle your finances. You're going to look at each liability based on its terms and in light of the entire situation. You're going to put on your thinking cap. Let's use my Spaghetti Table example as, well, an example.

Looking at each liability, here's what we see:

➤ **The Second Mortgage** payment terms are interest-only, so it has a nice low monthly payment. That's good for cash flow. It has a big balance. That's makes it tough to repay because it's going to take a lot of cash. It has a balloon in 2020, which is a while away, but it's also a bit scary because when it's due, something will need to be done. One other serious consideration is how attached I am to the house that secures this debt. If it's the home I plan to have forever and I'm very attached to it, it's important I get the business's success or failure out of the equation. I don't want to lose the house due to this one business venture. If

I'm not too attached to the house, this may not be a big factor for me.

⋏ **The Office Lease** has a few more years on it and then it's done. I can easily calculate my outstanding liability by multiplying the number of months left on the lease by the monthly payment. At this point, I have a gut feeling about the lease. I think when the term is over I'll want to move. Maybe I'll need more space, or maybe I'll need less, but no matter what I think will happen at the end of this lease, I will find a landlord that will lease to my business on the strength of the business itself rather than on my personal guarantee. I'll use my past positive payment history as an inducement. I may even be willing to pay a bit more in rent to be sure a personal guarantee is not required. Depending on the circumstances, I may be able to negotiate the removal of the personal guarantee for the balance of this lease that remains. (Strategies for negotiating with landlords and prospective landlords this will be discussed in Chapter 10.)

⋏ **The 2010 Ford F150** is used for the business. It's an integral part of the operations. It has a decent interest rate and a reasonable standard payment. There are only about 12 payments left to make. It's a secured item. That means if the payments aren't made, the lender will come take the truck. If the lender repossessed the truck and sold it at auction, they'd likely get less than what is owed so I'd be at risk for a deficiency judgment.

⅄ **The Bank of America Credit Card** has a large outstanding balance with a low monthly payment and zero interest. That makes it appear to be an economical way to have borrowed money for the business. However, when I look on the statement, I see that it will take 82 years to pay off this credit card if making the minimum payment. That's not going to cut it. Also, the zero-percent interest is going to jump to 28 percent in about a year. That is going to raise the monthly payment to more than double, or about $266, according to an online calculator.

⅄ **The Loan from Uncle Mortimer** is as free as money comes. He's a big believer in my business and wanted to help, bless his soul. I don't pay anything monthly and there's no interest. Maybe Uncle Mortimer is loaded and doesn't need the money to live. Or maybe Uncle Mortimer is a softy and loaned money he needs back rather quickly. He might be kind-hearted and will never bring up this loan over Thanksgiving dinner. Or, as much as I love him, he might lord this over me and make my life miserable until it's paid back. Whichever of those scenarios is the truth will affect my decision.

⅄ **The Outstanding Balance at Lumber-O-Rama** is from a previous job gone wrong in which I bought and used the materials but didn't get paid. As long as I'm making the $500 monthly payment, Lumber-O-Rama will continue to let me use the account. That's important to me because they're the best lumber yard in town and I need to continue to have a good relationship with them. At $500 a month, it will take me 10 months to pay and there's no interest charged.

You see now that we've looked at our sample that you really need to put on your thinking cap. This isn't a one-size-fits-all exercise. There are a ton of factors that will weigh in to your decision of how to put together your Untangling Plan. It's a good thing you are a clever entrepreneur, capable of creativity and complex thought, because you're going to need it.

Once you've really looked at each liability individually, you're ready to give each liability a plan and a priority. You can do that by duplicating your Spaghetti Table, renaming it The Untangling Plan, and adding two columns: Priority and Plan. Let's go back and fill in those columns in our example.

	The Untangling Plan				
Obligation	Outstanding Amount	Monthly Payment	Terms	Priority	Plan
Second Mortgage on Home	$30,000	$260	Interest only. Balloon 2/2020	High. I want to live in this house forever.	This is my highest-priority liability. I'm going to pay it off over the next 12 months via cash flow. If cash flow is insufficient, I will take out another loan to pay off this one.

Office Lease	[Number of months left multiplied by the monthly payment]	$3,500	Lease runs until 12/2016	Middle. I think I'll stay with this location into another lease term.	Negotiate with current landlord to remove guarantee for this term or the next.
2010 Ford F150	$8,000	$450	5%, paid off 10/15	Low	I'm going to continue to make the payments to retire the debt.
Bank of America Credit Card	$11,000	$110	0% interest until 8/14 then 28%	Middle	I'm going to use excess cash to make a dent in this debt

Loan from Uncle Mortimer	$10,000	n/a	Pay back when we can	Low	Uncle Mortimer is a kind and pleasant man who doesn't need the cash anytime soon.
Outstanding Balance at Lumber-O-Rama	$5,000	$500	No interest. Pay $500 until paid off	Low	I'm going to continue to make the payments.

As you can see, I gave each item a priority: low, middle, or high. All of the items on this list contain personal guarantees. Some are more dangerous than others. The priority puts into shorthand what you learned in your analysis phase, taking into account all the information you gathered and thoughts you had in the brainstorming phase. It feels nice to give everything its property priority because you can focus on the important stuff first.

Once you know the Priority, it's time for the Plan. How are you going to make this happen? What is the time frame? What's the plan to change the personal liability component?

Here are a few ways you can make the change.

⅄ **Profit.** Your Cash Flow Projection will tell you the profit your business is going to make in the next 12 months. You, as the owner, get to decide what to do with that profit. Removing risk from your personal life is a great way to allocate those funds. Take a look and see what liability you can retire.

⅄ **Change Your Cash Flow Projection.** As we discussed in Chapter 6, all the Cash Flow Projection numbers are flexible. Is there a way to change something to free up some money for The Untangling Plan? Would it be a better idea to wait on a big purchase and get rid of some risk here? Do you want to change your Owner's Withdrawal to make a dent in

The Untangling Plan? See what money you can free up by playing with the Cash Flow Projection.

⅄ **Find Some Money.** Is there an angel investor or venture capital in your future? Is there another Uncle Mortimer who wants to help? Do you have some savings that might be well spent here?

⅄ **Change the Equation.** You'll note in the Second Mortgage we plan to use cash flow over the next 12 months, but if cash flow is insufficient, we plan to get a different loan, even if that loan contains a personal guarantee. That's because the risk of losing a house we are very attached to is unthinkable. That has to change. Reducing the balance with cash flow and taking out another loan not secured by the house will remove the risk of losing the house, but not the personal guarantee. It's still a trade-off.

You'll notice that untangling requires negotiation skills, especially in the area of leases and when dealing with smaller, non-institutional creditors such as family, friends, and suppliers. Chapter 9 will give you detailed negotiation strategies to help pull this off.

⅄ ⅄ ⅄

The big payoff of The Untangling Plan is freedom. Your business needs to be completely independent of you. It can't rely on you for support. It needs to stand on its own two feet. Until that happens, you personally, and your family, will always be tied to the success or failure of the business.

As an entrepreneur, you need to be able to become wealthy independent of your business. Remember "The Donald"? He's wealthy regardless of what his individual businesses are doing. He doesn't put his personal fortune on the line for any one venture. As much as I hate to hold The Donald and his comb-over up as the bastion of anything, that's healthy entrepreneurship. That's financial savvy.

Chapter 8:

Fun with FICO

The biggest question I get via my Website and podcast is how to fund a business venture. Readers/listeners are looking for money to start up the business, to continue through tough times, or to launch the business to the next level. Money, or the lack of it, can determine the future of a venture. Many entrepreneurs are not picky and are looking for *any* source of money to make the business fly. It's like kids looking for candy: they might have a favorite candy bar but when all is said and done they'll eat sugar right out of the bag if they have to.

There are many ways to rustle up the necessary cash. The first and largest decision is *mine vs. yours.* You can self-fund, or bootstrap your business, or you can look outside yourself for the money. Once you've decided to look elsewhere, you need to decide if debt or equity funding, or a combination of the two, is best for your business. Debt is, of course, taking on liability in exchange for funding. Equity is giving away a piece of the pie in exchange for funding. Both have their benefits and drawbacks. Neither is "right" or "wrong," and you can use a bit of both if you desire.

As soon as you go looking for your money, the interconnectedness of business and personal finances becomes readily apparent. Only long-established, successful businesses will be creditworthy on their own. For everything else, you're going to need to prove creditworthiness. This can even be the case in equity funding, which can appear to be counterintuitive since they're not lending you money. They want to know how you treat money, and a credit report is their data point. For people giving you money either for debt or equity, it matters. Credit reporting agencies and credit scores (a.k.a. FICO) are major players you must understand.

Your Personal Credit Report and Score

Interestingly, not all countries even have this system of credit reporting. When I lived in the Czech Republic from 2004 to 2009, no such system existed. It was up to the individual bank to determine if you were worthy of credit. Your relationship with the bank, the stability of your employment, and the amount of cash you had determined your thumbs up or thumbs down. As a result, there were fewer defaulted loans, but much less credit was available. For now, in the United States, our credit score matters. Because you're likely more familiar with personal credit records and scores, we'll start there and then extrapolate that information to the business front.

There are three credit reporting agencies: Equifax, Experian, and TransUnion. They collect and maintain a history of your dealings with lenders and creditors; public records such as bankruptcies, judgments, and liens; and collections. FICO, whose full name is Fair Isaac Co., takes the information in one of your credit reports (any one of the three) and gives you a score somewhere between 300 and 850. A score of 760 or higher is considered high. FICO is not the only game in town, but it's the most prominent. So that means there are really two elements to your creditworthiness:

1. Your history with lenders and creditors, public records, and collections
2. The score generated based on your history

If the history is wrong—in other words, a company has reported something incorrectly or the credit reporting company has confused you with someone else—the FICO score will be affected. So step one on the way to great credit is to always be sure the underlying information is correct.

Your FICO score is the shortcut way for lenders to determine if they think you're creditworthy and how high their risk will be in lending to you. The thought process goes, if you've been good with credit in the past, you'll be good in the future. The FICO score is the easy way to determine that. Where it gets really interesting is that FICO uses special secret methods to determine your score. They tell us *what* goes into determining your score, but not exactly *how* it's determined. It's their secret sauce. They do tell us:

- ▲ 35% is your payment history. Did you pay your creditors on time? How have you handled credit in the past?

- ▲ 30% is the amount owed. What amount of available credit is being used? How many accounts do you have?

- ▲ 10% is new credit inquiries. Are you a credit collector? Are you amassing many accounts?

- ▲ 10% is the mix of accounts and types of credit. Whom do you owe? Can you handle different types of loans?

FICO mixes in all those factors using a special algorithm put together by super math geniuses and assigns you a number between 300 and 850. That number can be different with each of the three credit reporting agencies because they might all contain slightly different information, but they will be pretty close. That number is your personal score. If you're personally guaranteeing a loan, that score will be relevant because the creditor will be looking to you to make the payments. If you have a bad history or a low score, the money might not be available or it might cost a lot more.

How Your Business Interacts with Your Personal Credit Report and Score

Your personal financial health is of great interest to potential creditors, as we've seen when discussing personal guarantees. Creditors look to your personal credit report and use your personal credit score when determining *if* they will extend you credit, the amount of credit they'll extend, and the terms of the credit they're extending you. When an account is personally guaranteed, it is not only a business debt, but a personal one as well. In allowing the personal guarantee, you've given permission for it to be reported on your personal credit report. The history of the debt can now be reported on your credit report and used as an element of your score.

Interestingly, business accounts are often not reported on your personal credit report unless they become delinquent. This means that you won't get the positive benefits and boost to your FICO score, but you will get dinged if you miss payments or go into collections. Individual bank policy determines how banks report these items. Banks and lenders are not required to report this type of debt as they would a solely personal debt. Not all banks have the same policy on this, but this appears to be the trend. Even if they've used your personal credit in their determination of whether or not to issue the credit, banks don't report business items backed by a personal guarantee, unless you fail to pay.

Another little oddity is that the credit reporting agencies and FICO do not make any distinction between a personal item and a business item. Once the item is on the credit report (likely after it is a negative if it's a business account) it does not matter if the debt is solely for business purposes. It will be given the same weight as any other debt. Be aware, however, that a debt containing a personal guarantee is still a full-fledged debt. It will still be collected against in the same fashion as described in Chapter 7. Don't be lulled into forgetting about the seriousness of the personal guarantee just because you don't see it on your personal credit report. It still exists.

Your Business Credit Report and Score

We now know how credit reports work and what elements go into our personal FICO score. We also know how the credit reporting agencies and creditors treat personal guarantees. Now let's look at the business side of credit reporting. Did you know that your business has a credit report, or, if it doesn't, that it can? A little-known secret of the small business community is that your business can have a credit report, and you can derive great benefit from it. In fact, the credit report is held by the very same people who hold your personal credit report: Experian Business and Equifax Business, along with a few others, such as Dun & Bradstreet, Business Credit USA, Cortera, and Small Business Exchange.

Business credit reports are based on your EIN, or Employer Identification Number. You don't need employees or a particular entity to have one of these numbers; a sole proprietor working alone can get one. An EIN is available free from the IRS and you can use it to establish a separate bank account for your business. As an additional benefit, you won't be giving your Social Security Number (SSN) out to everyone and their brother who deals with you in your business. This will help keep your SSN more secure, and you'll look much more established using an EIN. You'll need an EIN to have a business credit report just like you need a SSN to have a personal one.

The Benefits of Having a Business Credit Score

Similar to having a high FICO score and a positive personal credit report, a good business credit report and credit score gives you many benefits:

- ⅄ Lenders offer better terms to businesses with high credit scores. This is money in your pocket via reduced interest rates.

- ⅄ You have the potential to avoid personal guarantees with a high credit score. The business is more likely to be able to borrow money on its own merits without you backing it up. You know how happy this makes me.

- ⅄ You have more choices, just like on the personal side. The better business credit you have, the more options you have for finding funding for your business. This makes you more competitive in the marketplace.

- ⅄ With a business credit line not attached to you personally, you can request cards for your employees. You can control their ability to spend by adjusting their credit limits.

- ⅄ You can protect your personal credit report if something happens to your business. This is the idea again of not sinking or swimming together. With a separate credit report, you can decide where you want to take the hit on your credit if the time comes.

What's in a Business Credit Report

Business credit reports are the same concept as a personal credit report, but they look a little bit different. They contain only information relating to the business. You'll find some crossover from your business to your personal credit report, but not vice-versa.

Here's what you'll find on the report:

- ⅄ Address and phone number
- ⅄ Key personnel and their titles
- ⅄ Family linkage (in other words, parent, subsidiary, and branch information)
- ⅄ SIC and NAICS codes to identify your industry
- ⅄ The year the credit report was established
- ⅄ Number of years in business, number of employees, and total sales
- ⅄ Information about debts, court judgments, tax liens, and bankruptcies with all the detail contained in a personal credit report

Most importantly, the credit report will contain a credit ranking between 1 and 100, from highest risk to lowest risk; the higher the number, the better. The 1–100 number shows what percentage of businesses score worse than yours. The score is calculated using yet another super-secret algorithm that takes into account the number of accounts, their balances, payment history, and trends through time. The algorithm will also factor in any public records information such as liens, judgments, and bankruptcies. Lastly, it will take into account the number of years you've had a credit report, the type of business, and the business size.

If you want to see a sample Experian business credit report, you can go to *http://emilychasesmith.com/ samplebusinesscreditreport*.

Getting Your Own Business Credit Report

The best way to know if you have a credit report already in place is to do a search with your company name and EIN. If you don't have a business credit report, the easiest way to start one is to get a DUNS number, issued by Dun & Bradstreet. You can find the link to get one here: *http://emilychasesmith.com/ getadunsnumber*.

Once you've established a business credit report, your next step is to start filling it. Similar to your personal credit report, it's useless without any information. This is going to take some effort because not every creditor reports business debt to the credit reporting agencies. In fact, Experian says that of 500,000 suppliers extending credit, only about 10,000 report.[1] As you build your business's creditworthiness via your report, you are going to want to work with creditors that report, because if it's not on the report, it's not going to be factored into the score. You may be allowed to supplement your business credit report with additional information when applying for a loan or line of credit, but your history holds more weight if it's all verified by the credit reporting agencies. When you're ready to grow, you're going to want a solid report.

Maintaining Your Credit Scores

Like a spare tire when you've taken on a nail in the middle of the Mojave Desert, you want your credit reports, both personal and business, to be there when you need them. Spare tires don't just appear, and neither do strong credit reports. You need to check both reports (a) yearly, (b) when you think there may be an issue, and (c) before you think you may need them. You are entitled to one free copy a year of your personal report, but you're going to have to pay for your business report. Once you get your hands on your business credit report, you need to do two things:

1. Make sure the information is accurate and up to date.

2. Make sure everything that can be reported is reported.

If your score is lower than you'd like, hatch a plan to improve it.

If Your Credit Is Crummy

It's all fine and nice to talk about credit reports and credit scores in the abstract, but what if your credit has taken some hits? What if it has suffered a tsunami? Should you skip this section, throw your hands up in the air, and resign yourself to credit purgatory?

Nope. Credit is not the be-all end-all. It's nice if you've got it, and it provides a lot of great benefits, but it's not a must-have, like air or water. It's more like a warm cooked meal. You won't starve without one as long as you have *something* to eat while you aspire to it. (As long as you have some granola bars out on the trail you won't starve while you're on your way to the inn.)

All the factors that go into creating your personal FICO or your business credit score are the very same ones that will tank that score. For example:

⋏ Late payments, missed payments, or default-ing on a debt

⋏ Using up all or most of your available credit

⋏ Rapidly applying for new credit sources, sig-naling you're desperate and likely to default

⋏ Tax liens, judgments, or collection action

The key to improving your credit is to let the bad items fall off your report and fill it with good ones.

As you become more financially savvy, your credit will improve. All the negative things on your credit can be corrected in time. Nothing is permanent. Here are the general guidelines for how long different types of reporting stay on your credit report and affect your score.

- Good stuff can stay forever.
- Past due accounts stay on 7 years from the date they became past due.
- Late payments stay on for 7 years.
- Collection accounts stay on for 7 years from the date they became past due.
- Settlements stay on for 7 years from the date they became past due.
- Judgments stay on for 7 years from the date filed, paid or not.
- Paid tax liens stay on for 7 years from the day they were paid.
- Unpaid tax liens stay on forever.
- Bankruptcies (Chapter 7, Chapter 11, or non-discharged Chapter 13) stay on for 10 years from the date filed.
- Discharged Chapter 13 bankruptcies stay on for 7 years from the date filed.

Business credit reports are a bit different. The general guidelines are:

⋏ Trade data stays on for 36 months.

⋏ Bankruptcies stay on for 9 years and 9 months.

⋏ Judgments stay on for 6 years and 9 months.

⋏ Tax liens stay on for 6 years and 9 months.

⋏ Collections stay on for 6 years and 9 months.

So, even though the time frames are long, bad credit isn't forever. In fact, if you pack good stuff on top of it, the bad marks lose potency in time as well.

I do want to take a minute to remind you that an item being *on your credit* is different from *being collectable*—in other words, a creditor suing you for the amount owed. As we've seen, sometimes the debt itself isn't reported. Also, the type of debt, the contract between the parties, and the Statute of Limitations on that type of debt in your state will control whether the debt is collectable, even if it does appear on your credit report. Being on a credit report and winning in court are two different things.

For those with bad credit, there are two concerns:

1. Improving your credit
2. Functioning in the meantime

Improving your credit consists of cleaning up the outstanding items. Chapter 10 of this book is devoted to showing you exactly how to do that. Once debts are satisfied and that satisfaction is reported, you then start stacking good on top of the bad. You layer as much good credit mojo over the bad old stuff as you can and your credit score gradually rises. This works even if you have a bankruptcy on your record. The older something is, the less weight the super-secret algorithm gives it. If you have bad old stuff with less weight and good new stuff with more weight, your score will rise.

Some good new stuff you can add to your credit includes:

- ⅄ Making sure you're Johnny on the Spot when making each payment
- ⅄ Adding a different type of loan to your portfolio, such as a home or car loan or a credit card
- ⅄ Paying down balances
- ⅄ Keeping balances low
- ⅄ Using an older existing account again

Credit Repair Agencies

Credit repair agencies are the snake oil salesmen of the 21st century. They are full of promises and hype but are very short on delivery. Even the Better Business Bureau says, "The truth is, no one can legally remove accurate and timely negative information from a credit report."[2] They'll take your money and leave you empty-handed. They have all types of schemes. The legitimate ones ask the creditors to substantiate their reporting.

The illegitimate ones can have you do things that are illegal like creating a new credit identity. Credit repair agencies don't have a magic wand or secret sauce. The way to get better credit is just as we've described: clean up the bad stuff and add good stuff.

> **Note:** Credit repair is different from credit counseling, which can help you come up with a plan to manage your money. Be careful here because many times credit repair masquerades as credit counseling. You might find a wolf in sheep's clothing. It's a rough-and-tumble industry and many people want to take your money. Make sure you know exactly what you're getting and how it works.

Creativity

In bad-credit land, we're going to work toward improving our credit and we're going to continue to function in the meantime. You're going to need to be creative. Good thing creativity is a core skill of an entrepreneur. You can either get creative with how you are going to acquire cash or you can get creative with how you are going to run your business with less cash.

Necessity is the mother of invention, and many of the most successful companies have faced the dilemma of where to find money. Apple didn't start out of garage because Steve Jobs and Steve Wozniak liked sniffing gas fumes; it was of necessity. In fact, some experts believe that too much capital is toxic to a business. With too much money you're not disciplined early on and you spend money before you are really ready to scale an idea. It's like an 18-year-old getting a large inheritance. It will soon be gone with not a lot to show for it.

Finding financing that makes sense for your business is a matter of balancing a precious ecosystem. Finding the right amount, under the right structure, and for the right price is a challenge, but it's just one of many you'll face and overcome in making your business thrive.

Chapter 9:
Negotiation Strategy When Haggling Give You Hives

When we lived in Prague, we spent two weeks in Hurghada, Egypt. Czechs, Germans, and Russians use Egypt for a break from the cold the way the Americans use Hawaii. In Egypt you haggle for everything—literally everything, from taxi rides to souvenirs. You even haggle somewhat with the guys who save tables at dinner and chaise lounges by the pool. I do not enjoy this process. I much prefer the U.S. method whereby the seller sets a price and we can pay or not pay as we decide. But when in Egypt, you must do as the Egyptians do.

Similarly, negotiation is a required skill in business, and failure to have that skill is to ensure you are ripped off around every corner and have nowhere to sit by the pool. You may find yourself negotiating:

- ⋏ Terms with a supplier or vendor
- ⋏ A personal guarantee on lease or loan
- ⋏ Compensation for a staff member or independent contractor
- ⋏ Buying or selling something big

These items are all directly related to cash flow, cash flow projections, and your Untangling Plan. Imagine the difference to the bottom line if you got just a better deal in a few key areas. Imagine the risk you can avoid via personal guarantees with strong negotiating skills. A few principles and guidelines on effective negotiation will serve you well on your journey to financial savvy.

Laser Focus

There are many schools of thought on negotiation and many great books written that delve heavily into that art. If this is subject of interest to you, you can make a graduate-level study of it. But for the purpose of becoming as financially savvy as possible, we will employ a laser focus on tools and tactics that will serve you in the negotiations you'll need to engage in.

From the outset I will tell you that I subscribe to the school of honey rather than vinegar. Aggressive jerks circling like sharks may take down some prey, but they won't win the hunt year after year. The seals will get smart and avoid them like they sharks they are. If you're looking to build a business and accompanying reputation that will serve you long after any one particular deal or venture, you will do well to keep the golden rule in mind: Treat others as you want to be treated.

This doesn't mean you should give away the farm or assume the position of permanent doormat. There's a lot of ground between shark and guppy. Try to be a big, respectable, non-scary fish—a blue whale comes to mind. No one messes with a whale, but they don't go running when they see one coming. Whales are respectful, pleasant, and kind, but not to be trifled with. Let that be you.

Preparation and Guiding Principles

Have you ever been caught off guard? I remember my sister mentioning at a Mother's Day gathering that she was thinking of selling her bike. This was a really cool beach cruiser bike, white and pink with a basket in the front. Its name was Betty. As soon as she mentioned she wanted to sell it, I was right there asking how much. By the end of the day, the check was written and the bike was relocated to its new home. As Betty drove away, I think my sister and I both wondered about the deal we struck. I didn't really know the value of the bike and I don't think she did either. If we had stopped and done a few quick online searches we both would have felt more confident about the deal (and after she reads this I'm sure I'm going to get an e-mail telling me to pony up some more cash).

My point is not to refrain from selling fancy beach cruisers to your sister, although that might not be a bad idea. It's to be prepared. Don't start a negotiation without knowing where you're coming from and where you want to go. Don't start an important negotiation just because the phone rang, you picked it up, and the other side is ready. Be ready yourself before you take the first step.

There are a few guiding principles that will serve you well as you walk through any type of negotiation:

- **Talk less and listen more.** The one doing the talking is the one giving away the valuable information. This may not be information that's necessary and/or secret, but it may give you vast insight into what the other party wants and how she views the negotiation. Give the other side the room to say everything she wants to and more.

- **Pretend you're asking for something for your mother.** It's easy to shortchange ourselves or think, "That's not too bad a deal." The question is, would you make that deal on behalf of your mother? Would you be happy with those terms for her? Or would you push a little further, spend some more time, get more creative for her? If so, know that your mother wants you to do that for yourself too.

⅄ **Let there be silence.** Pauses are not the kiss of death. Be comfortable with them. Many negotiators use pauses as a tactic. Don't be in a rush to fill them in. You never know what information you'll gain or what concession will be made in a pause.

⅄ **Be a broken record.** The pause exists at the opposite end of the spectrum from the broken record. Don't think saying something once is necessarily enough. Sometimes the other side needs to hear it again. Sometimes she needs to know it's important enough to you to say it yet again. Don't be afraid to go a little broken-record.

⅄ **Be careful what you put into writing.** When it's in writing, it's forever, so assume that's your final say on the matter. This is especially important when you start your contact via e-mail. It all feels informal and preliminary, but that is the other side's impression of you. It's also archived in her database and backed up, preserved for all posterity. Be sure you mean what you write.

⋏ **Know what's a win for you.** This is that idea of the super-cool bike sale. Before you enter into even preliminary negotiations, know your position. Know the terms that work for you. Know the extras you'd like but can live without. Know your walk-away point. Know yourself, because the other side can make things not in your best interest suddenly look very attractive and reasonable.

Tools and Tactics

In the balance of this chapter I'm going to outline the best tools and tactics I've found that work in negotiating things of a financial nature. These tools and tactics are like arrows in your quiver. You're not going to fire them all at once, but they'll be there when you need them. Pull out the one you need and go to town.

In law school my Criminal Law professor was a former criminal court judge. As these things sometimes go, one who has practiced in a particular field may not be well suited to teach it. This was particularly true of this professor. The course grade was overwhelmingly weighted toward the final exam that consisted of a factual scenario from which we needed to identify which crimes may have been committed, and discuss them. I was young, dumb, and lost in that class, but I realized there were only a limited number of things the professor could test me on: crimes. I made and memorized a list of all the possible crimes, and during the test, I held up my mental list to the factual scenario and picked out the ones that fit. This is exactly what you can do with these negotiation tools and tactics. As you go through your negotiation, hold up the mental (or physical) list, see which ones apply, and use them.

1. Be a Person

If you've ever been in a networking group you've likely had this statement burned into your brain: "People do business with those they know, like, and trust." It's a cliché, but as with most clichés there's a lot of truth there. So be a person.

I love the story of Mark Zuckerberg's acquisition of Instagram. He did the deal at his house and had his lawyers sit inside watching *Game of Thrones* while he and Kevin Systrom sat outside eating steaks and ice cream. It's not that Mark hates lawyers (although he might); he just knows the power of people being people doing a deal together. It might have a $1 billion price tag, but in the end, it's still people.[1]

I was once on the phone with a potential joint venture partner who was an introduction from a mutual friend. Even though he's in New Jersey and I'm in California we discovered pretty quickly that he went to school in the same city my grandmother lived, Santa Barbara. Santa Barbara's a central coast city and has been promoted as the American Riviera. It's a city people love. That was an instant connection and we've gone on to do lots of fun things together.

The moral of these stories is, don't jump right in. Spend a little time getting to know each other. Be people first.

2. Ask, Ask, Ask

Another arrow in your quiver is the question. Ask, ask, ask, and let them answer. Don't ask with ulterior motives. Don't ask to make a point. Ask to find out, to discover. Use beautiful open-ended questions such as these:

- ⌃ Can you tell me more about that?
- ⌃ Could you give me a little more?
- ⌃ What does that look like for you?
- ⌃ What would that mean to your company?
- ⌃ Have you had a similar experience?

Pretend you're a therapist and the other party is your patient on the couch. What could you ask that would help him explain what's important to him?

It's interesting, we think we know what's important to other people based on what's important to us. We think it's all about money, but oftentimes it's not. There's a new phenomenon in my area, and maybe yours too, in the residential real estate market: Offers come in accompanied by letters and pictures. I was surprised at how effective it was. One of the letters we received on the last house we sold really painted the picture of how the buyers saw their family in our house and how much they loved it. In the end, we told them if they matched another offer's price we'd sell to them. My sister's letter to purchase a house was so compelling that the sellers took $10,000 less. She is an English teacher so all that writing practice is paying off.

The long and the short of it is, even in selling a piece of real estate—a numbers game if there ever was one—other factors are in play. If you can ask the right questions, you might be able to make the right connections and make the deal.

3. Do Your Homework

We talked about knowing your position and parameters before you open up negotiations, but you also need to know the market. What's standard? You may end up agreeing on something different, but it's helpful to know what's going on in the rest of the world in similar negotiations.

Another aspect of doing your homework is knowing the other party's position. Imagine you were looking at renting a piece of commercial real estate. You had done your research about the market and knew it was tough for landlords. You also did your research on this particular landlord and knew he had four buildings in your general area and they were about 50-percent vacant. Would that information be helpful? More helpful than just knowing it was a tough market for landlords? Yes, it would. That is a motivated landlord who just might forego a personal guarantee for a strong company or some prepaid rent.

If you can, ask around and learn what you can about the personalities involved. Is there one particular sales guy who seems to get better deals for his customers? Maybe he has a special relationship with the sales manager. Maybe he brings volume. Can you jump on that bandwagon? Sometimes the best thing you can do for your negotiations is to open them with the right person because of who she is and where she is connected.

4. The Whole Is the Sum of Its Parts

As you negotiate, keep in mind that price is not the only or even necessarily the most important element. Each piece of the agreement makes up the final contract, and each is a negotiating point. Consider:

- Price
- Quantity and quality
- Scope of work
- Terms
- Warranties
- Delivery schedule

- ▲ Time frame
- ▲ Incentives
- ▲ Concessions
- ▲ Additional perks

As you can imagine, some of these elements I listed so cavalierly can in fact be very complex. Quality, for example, might be an in-depth discussion in which you cast around for an objective standard.

As you move forward in talks, ask yourself where you can give or take on each of these elements. Can you get creative and meet the needs of all the parties by playing with the pieces? Can you trade one element that is less important to you for another that is more important? If you get stuck on one point in your negotiation, try compartmentalizing; in other words, put a pin in the disagreeable part and move on to on a different element. You may find that agreement in another area gets some momentum going and removes the blockage. You can reach a final solution by approaching it piece by piece.

Beware that shrewd negotiators can present elements in such a way that they appear carved in stone. Have you ever been presented a contract, beautifully printed on legal-sized paper in nice type? How about something that's "industry standard" or "something we've used forever"? That makes it sound non-negotiable. It appears that element or the entire contract is take it or leave it. That's the intention. Just because something's in writing or "standard" doesn't mean it's final. Everything is negotiable. You might not want to negotiate down at your local Best Buy, but by all means negotiate where it matters, even where it's already in writing.

5. A Break Is Your Best Friend

Understatement of the year: Negotiating can be stressful. A lot is at stake and these are not muscles we exercise often. Depending on what's at stake, the size of the deal, and the parties involved, negotiations can also drag on and on. When you're tired, take a break. Don't get burned out and frustrated and start talking crazy.

Think about dealing with your children. When you're tired, what happens? At my house, something's spilled and tears flow—theirs and mine. How do we counteract that? We take a break when we're close to the edge. Afford yourself the same luxury when you're negotiating. Now, it's hardly kosher to say, "I'm frustrated; you're driving me to drink. Let's take a break." Instead, how about:

- "We've had a great discussion. I'm going to go back to my office and think about what we've talked out. I'll reach out to you tomorrow."

- "Thanks so much for your time today. I have an advisor/mentor/investor I'd like to consult about this matter. Let me chat with her and get back to you no later than the end of the week."

⋏ "That's all the time I have in my schedule for today. Let me process what we talked about and I'll get back to you."

You're allowed to take a break, and you're benefiting not only yourself, but also the whole negotiation in doing so.

6. Be Willing to Walk

No matter the supplier, vendor, potential staff member, or landlord, he, she, or it is not the only one. It might feel that way, but it's not. They're not the only fish in the sea. Be willing to walk away. Don't fall in love. Know your bottom line and your deal-killers and respect them. Remember, you're negotiating for your mom. You're negotiating for the long term. You're negotiating to remove risk. This is important stuff. Never wave off the nagging thoughts in your mind with an "It'll be ok."

As a side benefit, you never know what might happen if you're truly willing to walk away. I can tell you that my office has received many a day-later phone call agreeing to the exact terms the other party said were a "no go" just days before. Stand your ground.

Final Things to Remember

As we close this chapter I hope you feel more ready to negotiate. Remember that this is a reference chapter. You've read it now, so you know what's in it, and it's there for you the next time you need it. Pull it out and arm your quiver.

Remember, you have something they want; that's why they're at the table. They may huff and puff, but they wouldn't waste their time if there wasn't a significant upside in it for them. They're there to close you. Let them, but on your terms.

Chapter 10:

Settling Debt for Pennies on the Dollar

In the last chapter we talked about how to be a negotiation rock star. Negotiation in Chapter 9 centered on:

- ⅄ Terms with a supplier or vendor
- ⅄ A personal guarantee on lease or loan
- ⅄ Compensation for a staff member or independent contractor
- ⅄ Buying or selling something big

Those types of negotiation will come across your desk early and often. In this chapter, I want to take the negotiation skills you gained in the last chapter and apply them to a different, less common, but very important subtype: debt negotiation.

As I've mentioned, my legal background has a strong focus on bankruptcy. It's an area of the law I love to practice because you can take someone in a tough situation and make his or her life better—that's not too common in law. More often both sides are just pummeling each other, and everyone comes out bloody with no clear winner. In my practice, I work primarily with small business owners who are deeply in debt and looking for solutions. One of the solutions, as an alternative to bankruptcy, is debt negotiation. This is the process of negotiating down debt to a level at which it can be paid off. This is a great option when you can pay something, but not everything.

Debt negotiation can be used when you owe a low level of debt to many creditors or a high level to just one or two. Anytime you've fallen behind—in other words, become delinquent—on a debt that's not secured to any asset like a house, car, RV, boat, or furniture, the debt can potentially be settled. The most common creditors for this type of settlement are of credit cards, medical bills, repossessions, personal loans, and payday loans. Debt settlement happens outside the court system and is at its essence an agreement between a creditor and debtor to change the amount and timing of debt repayment. Debt settlement can be done in a lump sum or via payments. This chapter will tell you exactly how to make it happen.

Note: *Debt negotiation* and *debt settlement* are synonyms. You may also have heard of *debt consolidation*. Debt consolidation refers to a scheme whereby you stop paying your debts and instead pay a lower monthly amount to a debt consolidation company. The idea is that the company saves the money for you, and once there's enough in your account, it settles the debts. It's generally a three- or four-year process. It's a decent idea that often fails in the execution. One of the major problems is that the industry attracts crooks. There's no professional licensing requirement, so a fly-by-night organization gets people to pay a lot of money, and then it closes up shop. In another rendition, most of the money you pay goes to their fees, and there's not enough left to settle the debt before the creditors get anxious and start pursuing you. The three to four years is up, the program can't be completed, and all the money you paid faithfully each month is gone. Debt consolidation is just not a safe way to go. Stick with straight debt negotiation.

Why Would a Creditor Settle?

I can almost hear the skepticism coming through the pages: *This sounds way too good to be true.* I'm telling you that you can pay less than you owe and the creditor will take it and walk away. It sounds a bit like fairies and unicorns. Let me tell you what's going on for the creditors that makes it attractive to them.

The long and the short is that a bird in the hand is worth two in a bush, even to a big, institutional creditor. When you get behind, the first thing creditors do is call. They call more than a teenage girl. The fact is, they're calling so often because it's the cheapest and easiest thing to do. If they can call and convince you to pay, the issue is handled and they're happy. If, after calling and calling, you don't pay, a creditor's next solution is a lawsuit by which they attempt to win a judgment. A creditor can't just reach into your account, garnish your wages, or use other legal means to get their money without a judgment. Judgments come from a court, and to get a judgment, a creditor needs to file a lawsuit.

A lawsuit sounds very scary and expensive doesn't it? It does to the creditor as well. It's not that creditors never sue, but the vast majority of creditors are not equipped to handle litigation themselves. They need a local attorney, licensed in the state where they must sue, which is generally the state you live in. Attorneys cost money. Working with attorneys costs time. It's a very ineffective solution for the creditor. Let's say everything goes as planned and the creditor gets its judgment. Now, with the judgment in hand, the creditor has to work with an attorney to try and collect from you. It may be, and often is, that the judgment is uncollectable. It's called trying to get blood from a turnip.

You could file bankruptcy and the creditor would be out of luck. You might not have any assets. You might not be employed. The creditor might not be able to find your bank account. There are a lot of "ifs" for the creditors, and their actual collection rate is low. Creditors, especially credit card companies, have a lot of bad debt on their books.

Is it starting to make sense why your settlement is the bird in the hand? It's not the full amount, but it's something, and it shortcuts all the craziness that may or may not get creditors the full amount owed.

> **Note:** All of this applies to accounts that are behind. Creditors won't settle debts that are currently being paid because you're already the bird in the hand. If you're paying the monthly payment, you're a dream customer. They literally have years and years of receiving checks from you—mailbox money, if you will. You have to be behind on the debt to settle it.

The Phone Calls

You've seen that creditors are not necessarily in the catbird seat. They hold a very tenuous position. Once you're behind, you're going to start getting calls. Those calls might be from:

- ⋏ Employees of the creditor in a collection department
- ⋏ An outside company paid on a percentage basis to collect for a creditor
- ⋏ A second or third tier company whose business is to buy bad debt for a greatly reduced rate and attempt to collect on it.

I'll let you guess in which of those categories we find the most ethical and humane people.

No matter who they are, the job of the collection agent calling you is to call people all day long and use their best efforts to try to get them to pay. Collection agents have quotas and generally work on commission, and depending on who they are, they threaten, they belittle, or they cajole. They'll say anything they think will cause you to cough up the cash. I had a client who was told the creditor was going to pull a U-Haul up to her house and take all her things to the pawnshop if she didn't pay!

Keep your wits about you and remember the rules of the game. You have something they want and it's just a matter of finding the magic number.

The Prep

At the beginning of every journey you want to know where you're going and what you have to do to get there. Honestly, this may require a bit of investigation. Perhaps you stopped answering the phone and opening the mail when things got tough. You may not have a solid idea of who owns the debts or what the balances are. It's not uncommon, but now that you're on the path to settlement, the first step is to get a good idea of what you're dealing with.

Go ahead and open the mail, listen to the messages, and make a simple list from the smallest to largest dollar amount. List each account number separately even if they're with the same company, because different accounts can be assigned to different departments. List the original creditor's name, the account number, the new creditor and its account number if applicable, and the contact information.

Now that you know what you're dealing with, let's look at what type of deals you can negotiate.

Lump Sum vs. Payment Plan

You can settle your debt for a lump sum: a specific amount of money you pay at one time to fully settle the debt. You can also negotiate a payment plan. The real deals are in the lump sum settlements. The creditor gets good money where it only had bad debt before.

The bad debt is off its books. It doesn't have to chase you down anymore. Creditors are much more motivated by lump sum settlements. Lump sums can be spread over a short period of time, usually no longer than three months.

Payment plans are a second choice. In this scenario you get a defined number of months, usually no longer than two years, to pay a defined amount. You want to negotiate a discount on the total amount owed, and interest should not continue to be added to your account. Beware of a certain animal that masquerades as a payment plan, but isn't. A creditor, especially a credit card, will ask you to pay a small amount, $25 to $50 a month, to hold your account open. They agree not to harass you or sue you in exchange for this amount, and promise that the account will not be sold or transferred while you continue to pay the small monthly amount. This is only a good deal for you if you're not in a position to settle the account now, but think you will be in the future. If you're ready to settle and the creditor is offering this small monthly amount, don't accept, and continue to push toward a full settlement.

Where to Get Money

Sometimes people settle because they went through hard times and got behind on payments, but are now doing better. If they can get a discount on the total amount owed, they can pay it off and go forward. They can't pay the whole amount, but they can pay some portion. Other times, people have been through tough times, and they are not really in the position to settle. In order to settle, they need to pull the money from somewhere. Settlement can still be a good choice even if it's a "robbing Peter to pay Paul" situation because you're getting such a good deal from Paul. It might be worth looking into a loan or bringing in an investor to be able to pay down debt at a discount. Also, settling debt does reduce risk to the business, and also you personally if the debt has a personal guarantee. Once the debt it settled, you don't have to be concerned about a lawsuit from a creditor.

A word of warning: Don't play with the Big Boys, the IRS or your state taxing entity, to make a settlement happen. Don't fail to pay estimated tax payments or payroll taxes; that's like cutting off your foot to avoid an ingrown toenail. Don't do it. Remember the IRS has more power than any creditor to make your life miserable.

Tell Your Story

You have the concept, you know whom you owe what, and you're ready to rock and roll. It's time to pick up (or answer) the phone.

Settlement is a game. Your job is to convince the creditor that what you're offering is the best they're going to get, and you're going to do that by telling a story. Creditors consist of people who understand the realities of collecting on past due debt. You're going to tell your story and make your case to them. You're going to help them see that settlement is a win for them.

The first part of your story is the struggle. Be factual and humble with a drop of humanity thrown in. You're not adversarial, you're just explaining that you can't make the minimum payments, but you're trying to get them something. You're doing everything you can to get them paid. It might sound something like this:

"I want to reach out to you and let you know what's been going on over here. Our business has gone through some tough times the last year. We had some quality control problems and lost our largest account. We're doing our best to fix them, but at this point we're barely keeping our heads above water. We haven't been able to pay many of our creditors, including you."

The key to a good story is volume—just the right amount. It's like hair gel: too little and you're frizzy, too much and you're The Fonz, but the right amount and you're lookin' good. When you outline your story, start where you need to. Where did the financial picture start to change, and why? What struggles have you had, in business or personally?

Did your competitors undercut you on price, cutting into your profit margin?

Did the work dry up for some reason?

Did you get a divorce, with all its associated costs and a drop in your income?

Did you have a medical issue that affected the amount you could work?

There's a story. Pull out all the little details that make it long and uninteresting and stick to the important pieces. You want to hold your listener's interest and make yourself sound as faultless as possible. You're going to tell this same story many times, to many different people. Every collection agent you talk is going to take notes on your story and put it in your file. Make sure you're always telling a consistent story with the same highlights. Give your listener a reason to settle.

Your journey will start with a phone call, and you're going to start with the person who answers the phone. Generally those people don't have the power to settle. They're the gatekeepers. Start the conversation with your story, then move to your offer.

"We did have a deal go though last month and we have $X available. I'd like to settle this account for that $X. It's not something that happens a lot and we don't anticipate it will happen again, but we'd like to make some headway with this amount."

When you pick your $X amount, here are some guidelines:

⅄ The older the debt, the lower the possible settlement.

⅄ Many debts will settle in the 70-percent discount range.

⅄ You can go up, and offer a higher amount, but it's tough to go down.

⅄ I like to start by offering 20 percent in a round number so I have some wiggle room.

The gatekeeper on the phone is going to hem and haw. She's going to tell you that amount is not nearly enough. She can't go to her manager with that amount. She may act insulted. That's okay. It's part of the game. You know that one phone call is not going to do it. This is a process of convincing your creditors it's the best they're going to get, and nothing gets that point across as well as a broken record—the same story, the same offer, over and over. At this point, the phone rep will likely put you on hold, speak to her supervisor, and come back with a high number. Now it's your turn to hem and haw. It's too much. You just don't have it. You remind them that you do have $X, but you can't get to $Y.

Now, if you're not in sales, I know this is going to sound weird: If you don't get the number you want, thank the person and hang up the phone. Remember, this is a game. You're going to roll the dice and continue around the game board. You're going to call back next week and do the same thing. Remember, "No" is not an answer. You're not saying "no," you're saying "not right now." Call back the next week and do it again. If you get the name and number of a contact, call him or her directly. If you can move up the food chain to a supervisor, call that person. Repeat your story, repeat your offer. If you don't like who you're talking to, hang up and call again. You'll likely get someone else.

The Document Request

For some creditors a story isn't enough, and they will ask for documents to substantiate the story. You may be asked for:

- ⋏ Tax returns
- ⋏ Profit and loss statements
- ⋏ Pay stubs
- ⋏ Bank statements
- ⋏ A personal budget

At this point the creditors are looking to verify your story. They're looking for a way to justify allowing you a much reduced amount. They're also looking for information they can use to collect if it comes down to it. Sneaky, sneaky.

Here's my advice on what to supply and what to hold back:

- ⋏ Hand over things that substantiate your story and help you paint your picture.
- ⋏ Redact (a fancy word for "black out") all details such as account numbers, addresses, and other account holders' names. You don't

want your creditors to have any more information than necessary that can be used for collection later.

⅄ Stall on anything that makes you look too financially healthy.

If a document a creditor has requested is complicated or you think would be a negative to provide, don't provide it. Tell the creditor you'll see what you can dig up, and just take your sweet time, all the while reiterating your offer. Give your creditors some information, but not everything.

In the past for clients, we've provided medical and age documentation when we didn't want to provide tax returns and pay stubs because the amounts were too high. We've provided a self-prepared business profit and loss statement instead of tax returns. We want to give the creditor something, but not anything that makes it appear as if the client can pay more.

The Multiple Creditor Advantage

Owing a lot of money to a lot of different people is usually not a good thing, but in the land of settlement it's an advantage. Add into your conversation something like this:

"In fact, I have six credit cards and a total of $53,000 in credit card debt. One of those accounts is with you for $17,000. I'm working hard to put together money for each of the creditors. I have $3,400 right now. I'd like to settle this account today. If we can't reach an agreement, I'll see if I can settle with one of my other cards."

You've been sweet as pumpkin pie, but the undercurrent is that the first creditor to take the $3,400 gets the deal. Beware, the creditor might try to make that $3,400 a first payment, but you're looking to completely settle the account, so that's a no-go. You want a full and complete settlement.

When to Pull the Trigger

Every company has a bottom line. Every company is different, and every company changes constantly. I'd love to publish a chart of all the creditors and the percentages they'll accept. No can do. There are a million factors, both internal at the company and specific to each individual you deal with. We've had some creditors we can't push down below a 50-percent reduction and some we've taken down to 90 percent.

My advice is that when the number makes sense to you, it's time to do the deal. It's the law of diminishing returns: Compare how much more you are likely to save compared to how much time, effort, and energy you will expend to achieve that lower number. The longer you keep the negotiation open, the longer you'll be in this process. It's a personal decision for you to make. I've given you some guidelines about where to start and where history has shown you're likely to end up. You can push as long and as hard as you think will give you results, but the old adage, pigs get fat and hogs get slaughtered, is true here. At some point you'll want to get back to business.

Finalizing a Settlement

The first rule is to never, ever pay anything without the deal in writing and in your hot little hands. If it's not in writing and you don't possess it, it didn't happen. The most important step is to have the exact agreement committed to writing. Once you reach a deal, the creditor will fax or e-mail the agreement in writing to you. Make sure it has the following elements:

- ⅄ It should be on their letterhead.
- ⅄ It should list their name and the original creditor's name (if different).
- ⅄ It should include the account number and everyone on the account.
- ⅄ It clearly states the settlement amount and the date by which it must be paid.
- ⅄ It clearly states that it is a settlement of the entire account.
- ⅄ It is signed by a representative and includes his or her title.

Never send any money until you have the written agreement in hand. Don't pay them when you make the agreement on the phone. Wait to get the agreement in hand, look it over, and then call in and make the payment.

Creditors are anxious to get their funds and will want to do a check by phone. This gives them electronic access to your account, and with that access they could deduct more than they are entitled to if they were unethical. Never allow this type of access to anyone but your original creditor (in other words, the bank or lender from whom you originally took out the loan). If the loan has been sold or is being collected by another company this is not a good idea.

For all other creditors and collectors, use overnight mail and certified funds to get money there. The extra fees are well worth avoiding the chance that your account will be cleaned out using a check by phone.

I'm sure I don't have to tell you not to send cash.

Keeping Records

Keep your proof of payment and the settlement agreement writing together in your files forever. Settled debts can sometimes be sold on the secondary credit market "accidentally," and then you're dealing with an attempt to re-collect. You need to be able to demonstrate clearly that the debt has been paid. If you can't, the debt may be collectable again. That would be a huge bummer.

Credit Recovery

No discussion of debt settlement would be complete without a view toward the long-term effect on credit. Remember, debt settlement is only possible with debt that is already behind, so you are already receiving dings to your score each time a payment is past due. This will be true of both your personal and business credit report if you've personally guaranteed the debt.

When a debt is settled, it is reported as "Paid by Settlement." That indicates that the debt is settled and closed, and the continuous negative reports will stop. The settlement will be on your record for seven years, and the credit scoring agency will factor in the settlement to your score. Although the settlement will be on your record for many years, you can effectively use the tactics in Chapter 8 to layer good credit mojo on top of the bad. Even then, it generally takes two years from the settlement for your credit to recover. It can be depressing to think about having bad credit for several years, but the impact on credit should never be an impediment to a good settlement. Let's look at some numbers.

- If you have $25,000 on three credit cards at an average of 15-percent interest and the monthly payment is $562 to remain current, you'll pay $30,724 in interest charges. You'll pay a final total of $55,724 to fully pay off the credit cards.

⅄ If you settle $25,000 at a 70-percent discount, you'll pay a total of $7,500. You will have saved $48,224.

⅄ Your credit will repair in two years after debt settlement. That means you gained $48,224 in your pocket as a trade-off for having bad credit for two years. That's more than $24,000 a year.

You could pay the additional $48,224 and keep your good credit for two years, or you could keep the $48,224 and take the credit hit. The choice is yours.

If They Went Straight to a Lawyer

Earlier in the chapter we discussed the tenuous situation a creditor finds themselves in when we don't pay. Their solution of a lawsuit to get a judgment to be able to collect is not a great one from their perspective, but it does happen.

Lawsuit

If you've been sued, that means there's an attorney involved for the creditor, so you need one too. Not fun, I know, but all is not lost. All the same principles of debt negotiation apply. The debt is still negotiable and you can still get a great reduction, you're just going to have to do it through your attorney while taking care of the logistics of the court case.

The absolute worst thing you can do is ignore a lawsuit. A lawsuit that's not answered is a lawsuit that's lost. Please, as soon as you get served with the lawsuit, find a good local attorney who deals in this practice area because the consequences can be severe.

Wage Garnishment

Wage garnishments are a specific amount of income from employment going to the creditor each and every paycheck until the debt, interest, and charges are satisfied. Wage garnishments can only be put in place after a lawsuit that has resulted in a judgment.

If you have a job outside the company, or perhaps a spouse was on the loan with you, this can happen. In the state of California, the creditor can take 25 percent of your take-home pay to satisfy the judgment. That's a big chunk. You're going to want an attorney involved to attempt to stop the garnishment and come to an agreement. Depending on your financial situation, this may be the point at which you consider bankruptcy. We're going to talk about when bankruptcy might be the best course of action in Chapter 11.

Liens

These too happen only after a lawsuit. Liens can be against you personally, against the business, or against a specific piece of real or personal property. Liens have to be paid before you buy or sell most anything. They will also appear on your credit report. Liens generally do not provide the creditor money currently, but rather it holds a creditor's place in line to be sure it will get paid when you do. This means the debt is still ripe for settlement. The bird in the hand analysis still applies. However, depending on the laws of your state, the character of the property, and your financial situation as a whole, liens can also be used to force the sale of property to satisfy the lien. You need an attorney to know if this is the case. As with wage garnishments, you need the help of an attorney to settle the underlying debt and remove the lien.

Bank Levy

This is a scary one because with a bank levy, the money just disappears from your account. Yikes! This happens when a creditor has won a lawsuit, has a judgment, and knows where you bank (maybe because you've paid them out of this account in the past). It could also be the IRS or your local state tax authority (they don't have to have a judgment).

If a creditor has pulled money out of an account, don't put any additional money into this account.

Think like Jason Bourne: this account has been compromised. Stop all automatic payments and withdrawals to the account. A creditor can continue to tap into this account until the full amount of the judgment, plus costs, is paid. Now that they know where you bank, they'll go back to the well time and time again.

You need to consult with an attorney for a bank levy as well—and quickly. There may be a trick or two that will be helpful, and you need assistance with the balance owed to the creditor. We had a client who lost $62,000 to a bank levy and we were able to bring about $30,000 of it back to him. You need to know what, if anything, can be done. The least helpful solution is to try and go off the grid. You don't want to pay cat and mouse with the creditor, always trying to stay one step ahead. You want to clean up the mess and get on with your core business.

Wrap Up

No one wants to be in the position where they can't pay what they owe. It's a terrible feeling, but knowing you have debt settlement as an option can change the game and get you back on your feet quickly.

Chapter 11:
When All Else Fails, Raise the White Flag

One of the hallmarks of a financially savvy entrepreneur is knowing when the gig is up and when it's time to raise the white flag.

I understand how un-fun it is to struggle and how horrible it feels when that struggle looks like it will end in failure. It feels like the opposite of financial savvy. You just want to crawl into a hole and never come out again. It feels so huge, so public, and so permanent.

Bankruptcy Primer

Before we can go too far, we need to be sure we're all on the same page. Most people have at best a vague and general idea of what bankruptcy is, and a lot of misinformation abounds. In essence, bankruptcy is a financial do-over that gets rid of particular types of debt if you qualify. The debt can be wiped away, "discharged," or reorganized. You're crying "uncle" and asking for a fresh start. Bankruptcy is an actual federal court filing, and the law supporting it is fairly complicated. Bankruptcy is like a root canal: it sounds horrifying, but sometimes nothing else will bring relief.

Bankruptcy law is divided into chapters. Think of them as names for the different ways the law can operate, like different highways. They are:

- **Chapter 7** is the chapter most people think of when they think of bankruptcy. It's called the "liquidation" chapter. The simplified version is that the court will take much of what you own to satisfy what you owe. All other qualified debts will be discharged.

- **Chapter 13** allows individuals to reorganize their debt. You will enter into a plan with the court wherein you pay a monthly payment based on your income and what you owe. At the end of three to five years, the qualified debt not paid using the monthly payment will be discharged.

⌄ **Chapter 11** allows for reorganization for businesses and individuals with too much debt for Chapter 13. It changes all the time, and currently stands at about $1.15 million.

There are some other lesser-used bankruptcy chapters, but these three cover 90 percent of all bankruptcies filed.

Bankruptcy is provided for in the U.S. Constitution in Article 1, Section 8, Clause 4, which allows Congress to create "uniform laws on the subject of bankruptcies" throughout the United States. Congress took the opportunity provided in the Constitution and created the first bankruptcy law in 1800. It's been modifying bankruptcy laws every since.

When thinking about bankruptcy, it's helpful to understand why a country would provide for bankruptcy as a remedy. In Ancient Greece, if a man owed money and could not pay, he, his wife, his children, and his servants were forced into debt slavery until the creditor made the money back with their physical labor. Later, debtor's prisons were the norm. But those remedies, even by the 1800s, were not particularly useful. I don't want the guy who owes me money living with me and cleaning my house and doing my laundry. Not to mention, these types of remedies wreak havoc on a person and family who has, generally through a series of unfortunate events, more debt than they can pay.

I have found that the need for bankruptcy always relates to one of the following situations:

⅄ **Career crisis**—a significant business downturn, job loss, underemployment, furlough days, or salary reduction

⅄ **Family crisis**—divorce or child health issues

⅄ **Medical crisis**—hospitalization, disability, or work injury

Often it's a combination of two or more. There are usually some poor choices woven in there, often related to housing and tied to the subprime fiasco, but for the most part, the apple cart tips because of a legitimate crisis.

The government provides for bankruptcy because everyone deserves a second chance, but it also specifically intends that entrepreneurs get another opportunity to create a business that generates income and employment. Imagine the chilling effect on our economy if every entrepreneur had to get his business right the first time or spend the rest of his life paying for it. What a waste of our country's most precious resource. It's better for all of us to give each other another chance. It's better that some debts not be paid than every debt be paid in full while the wheels of industry grind to a standstill.

We as a country want to propel those with the vision, the hustle, and the dream to start and push forward business. That benefits all of us.

Personal and Business Spaghetti

Due to the tangled-spaghetti nature of our personal money and our business money, for an entrepreneur, the financial struggle is usually both a personal and a business one. For example, there may be personal guarantees involved. It's likely a business owner has gone into debt in an attempt to float the business during tough times. With small-business owners, we're generally not looking at the business in a vacuum; we're looking at both the business and the personal. The solution sought must address both.

Often, if a business is in enough debt and doesn't have future prospects, we simply close it down. There's not a reason to take it through a bankruptcy. There's nothing to salvage and there are no assets to be distributed to creditors. The business merely needs to be closed down with the appropriate governmental agency and the creditors notified. Depending on the type of business, a new entity may be opened even as the old one is being closed. We see this a lot in the service industry. Let's say a carpenter had an LLC that struggled and took on a lot of debt. That LLC can be closed, but the carpenter/owner can continue to work. He may hire on with another company or open a new LLC without the encumbrances of the old one. There's nothing fraudulent about this type of transaction because the original LLC is really closed and no longer operational. The carpenter is permitted to continue to ply his trade.

If, on the other hand, you want your business to continue, you may want it to go through a bankruptcy. It will be a lengthy, complicated, and expensive proposition, but if it's a business worth saving, it might be worth the trouble. You may have heard of American Airlines, K-Mart, Pacific Gas & Electric, Chrysler, and Washington Mutual. They all filed Chapter 11 bankruptcies to restructure and reorganize so they could continue to operate. Chapter 11 allows companies to reduce what they owe and change payment terms in an effort to create a plan that allows them to survive. It's a long, expensive process, but there are some special provisions for businesses that owe less than about $2.5 million to allow the process to be a faster and less costly. Chapter 11 bankruptcy is a complicated animal, but companies do come through it and live to fight another day. The most common scenario is that the company is not worth the $25,000 in fees it will take to get through a Chapter 11 bankruptcy, and so it's closed.

Over on the personal side, however, the owner has taken on personal liability to such an extent that she is forced into personal bankruptcy. This is the part I hate. This is the slovenly teenager taking down the whole house of cards. This is Susan.

Personal Bankruptcy for a Business

The majority of business owners forced into bankruptcy due to their business qualifies for Chapter 7. That's good news because they can be in and out and onto rebuilding their credit and lives.

Chapter 7 is a personal bankruptcy, but it will also get rid of business debt. You will need to qualify based on income, and you really need an attorney to help you determine if you qualify. Typically, if the debts related to the business are 51 percent or more of your total debt, you qualify. We see this a lot with real-estate investors. They've used their own credit to buy a stable of properties, and when they add up the total amount of debt, including their personal residence, more than 51 percent of it is business related.

The goal of a personal bankruptcy is to let you move on. Here are the types of debts that are discharged in bankruptcy:

- Unsecured debt like credit cards, including all fees and interest and all collection accounts based on them
- Leases
- Medical bills
- Repossession deficiencies

- ▲ Judgments (except in some circumstances such as drunk driving or willful or malicious acts)
- ▲ Attorney's fees

Debts not dischargeable in bankruptcy are:

- ▲ Most income taxes (it's complicated)
- ▲ Spousal support, child support, or alimony
- ▲ Most student loans
- ▲ Court fines

If you have an asset that's secured by a loan like a car, RV, boat, furniture, or timeshare, you may have to surrender the asset and the loan obligation is discharged, or you may keep it and continue paying on it. It depends what the asset is and how it fits into your overall financial picture.

The Process

The process of filing for bankruptcy should always start with finding a qualified attorney. Remember our bookkeeper analysis. You should not be trying to navigate the murky waters of state and federal law. You should be focused on building your next venture and providing for your family. A bankruptcy attorney's fees are part of the cost of extracting yourself from this business.

Find an attorney who does bankruptcy and just bankruptcy. Debt negotiation is okay because it's the same genre, but don't go with a guy who does family law, criminal law, and will change your oil too. You want the guy who's in the bankruptcy court every day and knows all the players. He knows the rules backward and forward and what will fly in your particular courthouse. A good attorney knows the law; a great attorney knows the judge.

Your attorney will give you a new part-time job: to gather all the numbers and documents needed to prepare your bankruptcy petition. He's not asking for fun. He really needs what he says he needs. When the petition is ready, it's filed with the court. This is the most important line in the sand. Once your petition is filed, creditors can no longer call you or attempt to collect. All lawsuits are paused, as are all wage garnishments and bank levies. It's called an automatic stay and it remains in place as you go through the process. Your petition is assigned to a judge and a trustee. The trustee's job is to review your petition, make sure it's not fraudulent, make sure you qualify, and make sure everything makes sense. The trustee may ask your attorney for additional information.

Roughly 45 days from the day your petition is filed you'll have a court hearing. Although it will be at the courthouse and those federal courthouses are generally nice, it will feel more like going to the DMV. The hearing is called the Meeting of the Creditors, and it's with you, your attorney, the trustee, and any creditors who want to show up. It's an opportunity for creditors to ask you questions about your petition.

Generally creditors don't come to the Meeting of Creditors. Funny, huh? There's really nothing to talk about unless they think something is amiss with your petition. We usually only see creditors when there's a business deal gone bad or when an ex-spouse wants to tell the court about hidden assets. Most of the time the hearing is over in a matter of minutes. Your attorney will be there with you just in case.

After the Meeting of the Creditors your attorney may provide some additional documentation to the trustee, and when the trustee is satisfied, it's all over but the waiting. You'll have about two to five months to wait for your final discharge paperwork. Keep in mind that the automatic stay is still in place, so you don't have to worry about collections during this time.

Once you've received the final discharge paperwork, you have your "do-over" and you're free to go forward and rebuild your credit and your life. This would be a good time to review Chapter 8 on your credit report and how to make it shine. Even a bankruptcy won't kill credit for much longer than two years.

Common Misunderstandings

Here are a few common misunderstandings I'd like to be sure you're not laboring under as you consider bankruptcy as an option.

⚔ **You can't file Chapter 7 after the changes to the law in 2005.** This just isn't true. The changes to the law in 2005 added qualifications to filing for Chapter 7. The idea was to have more people repay a portion of their debt in Chapter 13. Often, business owners qualify for Chapter 7 because more than 51 percent of their debt is "non-consumer."

⚔ **You lose everything in bankruptcy.** This is the area where the federal and state aspects of bankruptcy law come together. States get to determine what you as a debtor get to keep in bankruptcy, and it's all over the map. Some states are generous, some are not. There's a long list of types of assets and the value of each type of asset you can keep. Some states, including California, have a wildcard that lets you keep whatever you want up to a certain dollar amount.

⚔ **If you file for bankruptcy, you lose your house.** Not necessarily. If you have equity in the house, that equity has to be low enough that you're allowed to keep it under state law. If you don't have equity, you need to be able to continue to make the payments as they are. Bankruptcy does not modify mortgage terms except in very limited cases.

⋏ **Discharging debt as to one person discharges it as to all.** Not so. If there are two people responsible for a debt and one files bankruptcy, the other person is still on the hook for the whole amount. We see this a lot in divorcing couples. One spouse will file bankruptcy and that will force the other to file because she ends up with the full weight of the debt.

⋏ **Second mortgages can be erased in bankruptcy.** This can only happen on the completion of a Chapter 13 bankruptcy and only under certain criteria. This can only happen in a Chapter 7 bankruptcy if you give up the house. If you give up the house, all the mortgages are discharged.

⋏ **You can keep certain accounts "out" of the bankruptcy.** Nope. A bankruptcy petition is a snapshot of all of your assets and debts. You have to list it all, and each creditor is going to be given notice that you filed by the court.

⋏ **Bankruptcy is public.** It's funny, bankruptcy is a public filing, so technically anyone can find it. However, as a practical matter, unless you're a celebrity, no one cares.

I've said it once and I'll say it again: Bankruptcy is like a root canal. It's scary as heck, but when you need one nothing else will do. And just like a root canal, you'll recover. I hope this chapter has taken some of the unknowns out of the equation and you can make an educated guess on whether your financial situation requires you to investigate this type of solution.

Conclusion:

You've Got This

I'm a big reader. I love books, but often at the end of a business book I feel a little...what's the word...*overwhelmed*. I feel as though I got a lot of good information, but that the execution of it is totally out of my reach and it's stressing me out just thinking about it.

But, as Dr. Leo Marvin advises in *What About Bob*, baby steps are the key. Just take baby steps. You're doing fine. You've got this.

Now that you're done reading the book, it's time to take action. Open your calendar and schedule in the following six things throughout the next few months:

1. **Choose an accounting software.** 15 minutes should be all it takes. I'm pretty sure you already have a gut feeling about which one would work best for you.

2. **Hire a bookkeeper.** Plan an hour to brainstorm and look for your most important team member.

3. **Do your runway calculation.** Give yourself one hour if you have some strong numbers in place already and three if you don't.

4. **Create a spaghetti plan.** Start with an hour and see how much time you need to finish it.

5. **Mine for P&L gold.** Set aside the same hour weekly for the next few months.

6. **Create an exit plan.** One hour should do it.

Just executing on those six things placed in your calendar throughout the next few months will grow your financial savvy by leaps and bounds.

While we're at it, let's inject in a little motivation past the joy that is financial savvy. What would make it fun? I personally love ice cream. I'm talking *love*. Anything done with some ice cream is automatically a little better. Ice cream doesn't really dovetail well with cleaning the toilet, but it would make any of the six things I just listed a ton better. What's your ice cream?

What do you love? What motivates you? Give it to your hardworking self.

As you work, always keep the goal in mind. You are pursing financial savvy because:

- ⅄ It will bring peace to your business and your life.

- ⅄ It will stop the sleepless nights and "oh crap" moments.

- ⅄ It will ensure the continuation of your business.

- ⅄ It will help you build wealth, and with the wealth, freedom.

With the goal strongly in mind, the path is easier to walk.

I wish you radical success in all your entrepreneurial endeavors.

Notes

Chapter 1

1. O'Connor, Clare. "Fourth Time's a Charm: How Donald Trump Made Bankruptcy Work for Him." Forbes.com, April 29, 2011. *www .forbes.com/sites/clareoconnor/2011/04/29/ fourth-times-a-charm-how-donald-trump- made-bankruptcy-work-for-him/*.

Chapter 3

1. Eha, Brian Patrick. "Daymond John of 'Shark Tank' on the No. 1 Thing Entrepreneurs Need." Entrepreneur.com, August 28, 2013. *www.entrepreneur.com/article/228102#ixzz2dlUZoXCZ.*

2. "Lottery Winner Statistics." Statisticbrain. com. *www.statisticbrain.com/lottery-winner-statistics/.*

Chapter 4

1. "Mc Hammer $33 Million 1991." February 11, 2012, News24by7.com. *www.news24by7 .us/2012/02/mc-hammer-33-million-1991. html.*

2. Grimm, Veronika, and Friederike Mengel. "Let me sleep on it: Delay reduces rejection rates in Ultimatum Games." Maastricht University *Meteor,* March 5, 2010. *http:// edocs.ub.unimaas.nl/loader/file.asp?id=1491.* See also *Economic Letters* 111.2 (May 2011): 113–115.

Chapter 8

1. "Why aren't all of my suppliers listed in my business credit report?" BusinessCreditFacts. com, A part of Experian. *www .businesscreditfacts.com/suppliersNonReporting .aspx?lsv=www.*

2. "Industry Tips: Credit Repair Companies." Arkansas BBB. *www.bbb.org/arkansas/ business-reviews/credit-card-processing-service/ industry-tips/credit-repair-companies.*

Chapter 9

1. Lynley, Matt. "Mark Zuckerberg Kept His Lawyers in His House While He Negotiated a $1 Billion Acquisition Outside." BusinessInsider.com, May 12, 2012. *www. businessinsider.com/mark-zuckerberg- kept-his-lawyers-in-his-house-while-he- acquired-negotiated-a-1-billion-acquisition- outside-2012-5.*

Index

About the Author

EMILY CHASE SMITH, ESQ., is the Entrepreneur's Money Expert. She is a California attorney with a long history of helping business owners and entrepreneurs make financially savvy decisions as they start, grow, and transition in their businesses. Money only counts if you keep it. She hosts "The Entrepreneur's Money" Podcast and blogs at EmillyChaseSmith.com.